The Present Future

The Present Future

Six Tough Questions
for the Church

Reggie McNeal

A LEADERSHIP ✳ NETWORK PUBLICATION

JOSSEY-BASS
A Wiley Imprint
www.josseybass.com

Published by Jossey-Bass
A Wiley Imprint
989 Market Street,San Francisco,CA94103-1741 –www.josseybass.com

Readers should be aware that Internet Web sites offered as citations and/or sources for further
information may have changed or disappeared between the time this was written and when it is
read.

Limit of Liability/Disclaimer of Warranty: While the publisher and author have used their best
efforts in preparing this book, they make no representations or warranties with respect to the
accuracy or completeness of the contents of this book and specifically disclaim any implied
warranties of merchantability or fitness for a particular purpose. No warranty may be created
or extended by sales representatives or written sales materials. The advice and strategies
contained herein may not be suitable for your situation. You should consult with a professional
where appropriate. Neither the publisher nor author shall be liable for any loss of profit or any
other commercial damages, including but not limited to special, incidental, consequential, or
other damages.

Jossey-Bass books and products are available through most bookstores. To contact Jossey-Bass
directly call our Customer Care Department within theU.S.at 800-956-7739, outside theU.S.at
317-572-3986, or fax 317-572-4002.

Jossey-Bass also publishes its books in a variety of electronic formats. Some content that appears in
print may not be available in electronic books.

Library of Congress Cataloging-in-Publication Data
McNeal, Reggie.
     The present future : six tough questions for the church / Reggie McNeal.—1st ed.
        p. cm.
     ISBN 978-0-7879-6568-6 (alk. paper
     ISBN 978-0-4704-5315-5 (paperback)
     1. Church renewal—United States. I. Title.
   BV600.3.M36 2003
   262'.001'7—dc21   2003011733

Printed in the United States of America
FIRST EDITION
HB Printing   20 19 18 17 16 15 14 13 12 11
PB Printing   10 9 8 7 6 5 4

Leadership Network Titles

Leading from the Second Chair: Serving Your Church, Fulfilling Your Role, and Realizing Your Dreams, by Mike Bonem and Roger Patterson

The Way of Jesus: A Journey of Freedom for Pilgrims and Wanderers, by Jonathan Campbell with Jennifer Campbell

Leading the Team-Based Church: How Pastors and Church Staffs Can Grow Together into a Powerful Fellowship of Leaders, by George Cladis

Organic Church: Growing Faith Where Life Happens, by Neil Cole

Leading Congregational Change Workbook, by James H. Furr, Mike Bonem, and Jim Herrington

Leading Congregational Change: A Practical Guide for the Transformational Journey, by Jim Herrington, Mike Bonem, and James H. Furr

The Leader's Journey: Accepting the Call to Personal and Congregational Transformation, by Jim Herrington, Robert Creech, and Trisha Taylor

Culture Shift: Transforming Your Church from the Inside Out, by Robert Lewis and Wayne Cordeiro, with Warren Bird

A New Kind of Christian: A Tale of Two Friends on a Spiritual Journey, by Brian McLaren

The Story We Find Ourselves in: Further Adventures of a New Kind of Christian, by Brian McLaren

The Present Future: Six Tough Questions for the Church, by Reggie McNeal

A Work of Heart: Understanding How God Shapes Spiritual Leaders, by Reggie McNeal

The Millennium Matrix: Reclaiming the Past, Reframing the Future of the Church, by M. Rex Miller

Shaped by God's Heart: The Passion and Practices of Missional Churches, by Milfred Minatrea

The Ascent of a Leader: How Ordinary Relationships Develop Extraordinary Character and Influence, by Bill Thrall, Bruce McNicol, and Ken McElrath

The Elephant in the Boardroom: Speaking the Unspoken About Pastoral Transition, by Carolyn Weese and J. Russell Crabtree

To the new tribe;
you know who you are.
May your tribe increase!
There's a world counting on you.

Contents

About Leadership Network   ix

Acknowledgments   xi

Preface   xiii

Introduction   xv

New Reality Number One: The Collapse of the Church Culture   1

New Reality Number Two: The Shift from Church Growth to Kingdom Growth   20

New Reality Number Three: A New Reformation: Releasing God's People   43

New Reality Number Four: The Return to Spiritual Formation   69

New Reality Number Five: The Shift from Planning to Preparation   92

New Reality Number Six: The Rise of Apostolic Leadership   120

Things I Didn't Say   140

Conclusion   146

References   149

The Author   151

About Leadership Network

Since 1984, Leadership Network has fostered church innovation and growth by diligently pursuing its far-reaching mission statement: *To identify, connect, and help high-capacity Christian Leaders multiply their impact.*

While Leadership Network's techniques adapt and change as the Church faces new opportunities and challenges, the organization's work followes a consistent and proven pattern: Leadership Network brings together entrepreneurial leaders who are focused on similar ministry initiatives. The ensuing collaboration—often across denominational lines—provides a strong base from which individual leaders can better analyze and refine their individual strategies. Peer-to-peer interaction, dialogue, and sharing inevitably accelerate participants' own innovations and ideas. Leadership Network furthur enhances this process through the development and distribution of highly targeted ministry tools and resources—including audio and video programs, special reports, e-publications, and online downloads.

With Leadership Network's assistance, today's Christian leaders are energized, equipped, inspired, and better able to multiply their own dynamic Kingdom-building initiatives.

Launched in 1996 in conjunction with Jossey-Bass, a Wiley Imprint, Leadership Network Publications present thoroughly researched and innovative concepts from leading thinkers, practitioners, and pioneering churches. The series collectively draws from a wide range of disciplines with individual titles providing perspective on one or more of five primary areas:

- Enabling effective leadership
- Encouraging life-changing service
- Building authentic community
- Creating Kingdom-centered impact
- Engaging cultural and demographic realities

For additional information on the mission or activities of Leadership Network, please contact:
Leadership Network
www.leadnet.org
800.765.5323
client.care@leadnet.org

Acknowledgments

Many people have contributed to my thinking through the years. As I have formulated my convictions about the missional expression of the North American church in the emerging world, the following people have been most formative for me: George Barna, Warren Bennis, Peter Drucker, Bill Easum, Findley Edge, Carl George, George Gilder, Gary Hamel, Charles Handy, Lyle Shaller, Howard Snyder, and Len Sweet. What makes sense to the reader in these pages is their contribution: the rest is mine.

I am grateful to Carol Childress (Leadership Network) for the encouragement to put this down in print and to Mark Kerr (Jossey-Bass) for his enthusiasm for the project and editorial assistance for light-speed production.

Finally, the three women of my life continue to provide constant inspiration. Cathy, my soulmate and prayer champion, believes for me when I can't. Jessica and Susanna, my two teenage daughters, excite my efforts to challenge the church. I want them to experience a vibrant, missional Christian movement in North America.

Preface

We think we are headed toward the future. The truth is, the future is headed toward us. And it's in a hurry (we now know the universe is speeding up, not slowing down). We also generally think that the present makes sense only in light of the past. Again, we need to check our thinking. The present makes clearest sense in light of the future. We humans write history by looking at the past. God creates history ahead of time. He never forecasts. God always backcasts. He began with the end in mind. The future is always incipient in the present. Before the foundation of the world, the Lamb was slain. Calvary was anticipated in God's kiss of life into Adam. The cross gains dimension silhouetted against the empty tomb. The empty tomb confirmed the invasion of the future into the present. When Paul encountered the resurrected Jesus, he realized the future had been fast-forwarded. That changed everything.

It still does.

Introduction

This book may not be for you. Not that long ago, it wasn't for me either. In fact, I am not thrilled about writing this book for several reasons. One is that I am afraid that I will fail to communicate well enough what I want to say about how desperately we need to make some changes. Another is that you won't be able to hear what I am saying because you are threatened by it or that you will shut down before giving me a hearing.

I also don't get kicks out of deconstructing a world I was once very fond of. It is a world that nurtured me when I was young and imparted the faith to me and has continued to confirm and legitimize my life calling. I grew up in the home of a bivocational pastor, whose dad before him was a mill village pastor, whose dad before him was a song leader and Bible teacher. My two older brothers are ministers; my two sisters both married ministers; a niece is married to a minister; a nephew is studying for ministry. I began ministry in the church thirty years ago as a college freshman. Ministry and the church have been my world. But it is a world that I increasingly find difficult to feel at home in because it lacks spiritual purpose and missional vitality.

I'm talking about the church world in North America. A world that has largely forsaken its missional covenant with God to be a part of kingdom expansion. It has, instead, substituted its own charter of church as a clubhouse where religious people hang out with other people who think, dress, behave, vote, and believe like them. This book will separate me from many people who are in that world who will never understand what possessed me to do this (or who may indeed suggest that something did possess me). I don't like rejection any more than the average emotionally needy person.

I believe there are many people like me in the church who, in terms of their church experience, want to script a story different from the one they are a part of now. I believe this because I talk with these people every day. My work carries me into dozens of congregations to meet hundreds of church leaders every year. In addition, I consult with denominational agencies, teach at seminaries, speak for parachurch organizations. In every arena I am running into an increasing number of people who are expressing fundamental doubts about the viability of the church. These are not critics from the outside who don't like what the church is doing. These are connected leaders who don't like what they are experiencing in church.

This morning I spoke with a young pastor who has hopes for the future of the church but is currently captive to club members in the congregation he serves. "I wonder why I am still doing this," he sighed. He's only thirty years old! Some of us are asking this question after many more years of investment. If you are, I am writing to give legitimization to your concerns and doubts about the church culture, but also to give you hope. **I want to help you by giving you ways of starting conversations that might lead you out of church captivity and into the adventure you anticipated.**

This book is not for you if you are content with the way things are. You shouldn't read this if you are just hanging on to your church job because you don't know what else to do. You should put this book down now if you can't separate faith from institutional religion or if you can't contemplate a God larger than your experience of him in your church tradition. By all means do not read this book if you are looking to bolster your opinion that the way to the future is charted through the past ("we just need to get back to . . ."). Please, if you fit any (or all) of these categories, take my advice and don't read this book. It will just agitate you. Trust me, you don't agree with it. Here are just some of the assumptions that are challenged in these pages:

- If you build the perfect church (the way we think about church), they will come.
- Growing your church will automatically make a difference in the community.
- Developing better church members will result in greater evangelism.
- The church needs more workers (for church work).
- Church involvement results in discipleship.
- Better planning will get you where you want to go (in terms of missional effectiveness).

If you believe these things, you are operating in a world that has a short time left. Even worse, if you persist in acting on these assumptions, you could actually hinder the current mission of God.

On the other hand, if you are convinced that God has not abandoned the world, you should read this book. If you have leadership responsibilities and want to challenge the people you lead to think through your ministry strategy, I think you will find help. If you are convinced that the new world is radically different but the church lives in a bubble world, you should get help here to understand more of what's going on (and why the church is increasingly irrelevant to people outside the bubble). If you are willing to ask different questions than most of the people in the church, you might be at home in these pages. If you are looking for costly adventure, this trip might be for you.

Let me be blunt. **I am writing this book as a polemical volume. I want to galvanize church leaders to action before it's too**

late. My goal is to provoke and to frame conversations that lead to action, to risk, to rediscovery of mission.

Many church leaders feel overwhelmed with the challenge of ministry in this new world. Maybe you are one. Perhaps you even know some of the contours of the emerging culture and some of the "hair balls" in the current church culture that prevent it from being missionally effective. But where do you start? How do you present a comprehensive agenda for missional rediscovery rather than introducing piecemeal approaches and ideas? How do you know the difference between fads and major changes? What is worth cashing in some leadership chips for? What will really make a difference in the long haul?

Church leaders have got to start working on better questions than we've been fooling with for the last half of the twentieth century. A lot of people have been saying for years many of the things you are going to read in these pages. **My hoped-for contribution is to provide you with a synthesis of essential actions, an overall strategy, which will help you move forward with those who will join you in reshaping the Christian movement in North America.**

I contend that a future already exists that significantly alters the spiritual landscape in North America. I identify six new realities of this present future that must be addressed by church leaders who want to participate in a renewal of the North American church. These realities represent tectonic shifts in the ethos of the spiritual quest of humanity. Even though they can be separated out for discussion, the whole set must be addressed if we want a full engagement with their implications. Each reality requires the church to shift its thinking from answering the wrong question to pursuing the implications of a tough question. The wrong questions reflect an approach to the future that focuses on solving yesterday's problems. **In my observation, most church leaders are preoccupied with the wrong questions.** If you solve the wrong problems precisely, what have you accomplished? You have wasted a lot of energy and perhaps fooled yourself that you have done something significant. Each tough question reframes the issue in a way designed to prompt discussion within you as well as between you and other leaders in your constellation of influence.

I have three target groups of church leaders I want to help. The first is congregational leaders who get it and are growing restless for something to happen that only God can get credit for. My second target group is pastors and staff leaders who already share the ideas I present but who need help in converting their leadership constellation. And I want to address emerging leaders, both clergy and lay, who are going to give leadership to the church in the emerging world.

This is not a how-to book. It will frustrate those looking for a "model" for doing church. I believe the search for models can often short-circuit a significant part of a leader's journey into obedience to God. The Bible is not a book of models; it is a record of radical obediences of people who listened and responded to the direction of God for their lives. The quality of leadership we need for the renewal of the North American church requires that we have people who are operating from a well-thought-out approach so they will know why they are doing what they are doing, not just copying someone else's cool idea.

That is why this book is not a travel brochure ("go here to see this"). When I give illustrations of leaders and churches who are operating effectively within these new spiritual dimensions, I deliberately don't give specifics. **I want to give you enough suggestion for you to prepare for your own journey. I want to get you in a position to hear from God by helping to create for you a new mental landscape as you listen and look for him.** Once you know what you are looking for you will find it (a lot of helpful travel brochures are being produced).

My life calling is to be a missionary to the church in North American to help it rediscover the mission of the church. This book is another way I am trying to be obedient to this assignment from God. It's a tall order because many, if not most, church members have never experienced missional living. They've just experienced church.

"Don't do it!" he said. I had just explained to a friend that I was writing this book. "It won't make many difference. The church is not interested in the truth." My friend has given up, defeated in his very public ten-year crusade to reform the church. He has taken his campaign in another direction. He may be right. I don't know. I may do what my friend has done eventually. But right now, like Jeremiah, I have to get this said—even though I know many will not listen or receive it well.

Because maybe it will help the church. Maybe it will help you. Above all, maybe it will help others become part of the kingdom of God.

The Present Future

New Reality Number One

The Collapse of the Church Culture

The current church culture in North America is on life support. It is living off the work, money, and energy of previous generations from a previous world order. The plug will be pulled either when the money runs out (80 percent of money given to congregations comes from people aged fifty-five and older) or when the remaining three-fourths of a generation who are institutional loyalists die off or both.

Please don't hear what I am not saying. The death of the church culture as we know it will not be the death of the church. The church Jesus founded is good; it is right. The church established by Jesus will survive until he returns. The imminent demise under discussion is the collapse of the unique culture in North America that has come to be called "church." This church culture has become confused with biblical Christianity, both inside the church and out. In reality, the church culture in North America is a vestige of the original movement, an institutional expression of religion that is in part a civil religion and in part a club where religious people can hang out with other people whose politics, worldview, and lifestyle match theirs. As he hung on the cross Jesus probably never thought the impact of his sacrifice would be reduced to an invitation for people to join and to support an institution.

We are witnessing the emergence of a new world. The church of Jesus is moving into the postmodern world. Its expression is going to be more different than most people realize or may want to imagine. The scale of the shift will rank along with the epochal transitions of ancient church to medieval, from medieval to modern.

This phenomenon has been noted by many who tag the emerging culture as post-Christian, pre-Christian, or postmodern. The point is, **the world is profoundly different than it was at the middle of the last century,** and everybody knows it. Even the church culture. But knowing it and acting on it are two very different things. **So far the North American church largely has responded with heavy infusions of denial,** believing the culture will come to its senses and come back around to the church. This denial shows up in many ways. Many churches have withdrawn from the community. An alternate form of denial has been the attempt to fix the culture by flexing political and economic muscle. Still another form of denial shows up in the church's obsession with internal theological-methodological debates designed to determine who the true believers are while the world is headed to hell in a handbasket.

All Is Not Well

If you don't need much convincing that the church ain't cuttin' it in terms of missional effectiveness, then you might want to skip this section. **This next stuff is for those of you who need convincing or who need ammunition for making the case to others.**

The collapse of the church culture can be demonstrated in several ways. One is through demographics. The percentage of Americans who claim to go to church each week has hung in the 40 to 43 percent range for thirty years. But I ask you, do you really believe those numbers? I recently asked a group of pastors in a conference setting whether any of them live in a community where 40 percent of the population shows up at church on Sunday. Only one raised his hand. A study conducted in the late 1990s suggested Americans might be lying about their churchgoing habits to pollsters. It pegged church attendance at only 26 percent of Americans. (The study was conducted by sociologist Stanley Presser of the University of Maryland and research assistant Linda Stinson of the U.S. Bureau of Labor Statistics, who assessed church attendance by actual diary entries as opposed to responses to pollsters.) Quite a difference! Think about it. Does your town even have room in all the churches for 40 percent of the population? A friend of mine in a Southern Bible Belt town called every church in his town after Easter in 2001 and reported that only about 25 percent of the town attended church—on Easter!

Let's say you do believe the church attendance that people report. There is still cause for alarm. **The further down you go in the generational food chain, the lower the percentage each succeeding generation reports going to church.** The drop is from the 52 percent of builders (those born before 1946) and seniors to only 36 percent of gen Xers. What does this spell for the church in the future? Armed with this information, of course, churches are launching an all-out effort to reach gen Xers. I wish! Most churches have actually just written them off, waiting for them to grow up and learn to like what the church has to offer.

Or let's take a look at the unchurched population. A 2001 survey reported in the *Christian Science Monitor* reveals that the number of Americans who have "no religious preference" has doubled from 1990 to 2001, reaching 14 percent of the population. (These are not skeptics—only 1 percent identified themselves as atheists. This group doesn't see the church as vital to their spiritual life.) George Barna reports (*State of the Church 2002*, p. 17) that the unchurched population has grown from 24 to 34 percent in just one decade! (Barna defines people as unchurched "if they have not attended a Christian church service during the past six months, other than for special events such as weddings or funerals.") Among some subgroups the increase is even more substantial. Since 1991, the number of unchurched women has risen from 18 to 30 percent; the number of unchurched Hispanics has jumped from 19 percent to 33 percent; the number of unchurched in the Northeast is up from 26 to 38 percent; and the unchurched population on the West Coast has risen from 29 to 40 percent. (If you've been in California on Sunday you may be suspicious that the reported numbers of unchurched are so low!)

For evangelicals, the situation looks even bleaker. Thom Rainer of the Billy Graham School of Evangelism at Southern Baptist Seminary reports some disturbing responses to the two frequently asked Evangelism Explosion questions ("Do you know for certain that if you died today you would go to heaven?" and "If you were to die today, what would you say to God if he asked you why he should let you into his heaven?"). The interview included about 1,300 persons of each of four generational groups that Rainer identified and investigated (5,200 in all). Analyzing the responses for evidence that the respondents were born-again (the evangelical definition of one's being a Christian) yielded the following results: builders (born before 1946)–65 percent; boomers (born between 1946 and 1964)—35 percent; busters (born between 1965 and 1976)—15 percent; bridgers (born between 1976 and 1994)—4 percent. Those interviewed in the bridger category were at least seventeen years old.

What about retention rates? Dawson McAlister, national youth ministry specialist, says that 90 percent of kids active in high school youth groups do not go to church by the time they are sophomores in college. One-third of these will never return. This rate of disconnection indicates a dilemma far more serious than mere youthful rebellion.

A growing number of people are leaving the institutional church for a new reason. They are not leaving because they have lost faith. **They are leaving the church to preserve their faith.** They contend that the church no longer contributes to their spiritual development. In fact, they say, quite the opposite is true. The number of "post-congregational" Christians is growing. David Barrett, author of the *World Christian Encyclopedia*, estimates that there are about 112 million "churchless Christians" worldwide, about 5 percent of all adherents, but he projects that number will double in the next twenty years!

The bottom line is that the bottom line is not looking too good, no matter how you cut it. Underneath the semblance of an American culture influenced by Christianity, the tectonic plates have shifted.

It's more than numbers. The American culture no longer props up the church the way it did, no longer automatically accepts the church as a player at the table in public life, and can be downright hostile to the church's presence. The collapse I am detailing also involves the realization that values of classic Christianity no longer dominate the way Americans believe or behave.

Sure, when there's a community disaster or a national calamity such as 9/11, people scurry to church. This is not because they have a sudden interest in church but because they have a huge need for God, and they still seek sacred spaces to pray. Some argue that these church attendance spikes reflect more peoples' need for community in times of shared grief than anything else. At any rate, within a few weeks of these disasters things are back to normal in terms of church attendance. The prognosticators who view these spikes as a renewal or beginning of a spiritual awakening remain frustrated. Most significant, a vast number of churches squander the window of opportunity by failing to connect with new people in these moments in meaningful ways that will bring them back.

The World Has Ended

We can place the enormous changes taking place against the larger landscape. We are entering a new epoch of human history called the postmodern age. The postmodern world will demand a new church expression, just as did the rise of the modern world. The church took years to accommodate itself to the modern world that adopted Galileo's and Copernicus's view of the universe (deposing God from his fixed, top-of-heap position) and embraced Cartesian logic (pushing God to a diminishing domain of what could not be explained away by reasoning).

The modern world assaulted God, shoving him further and further into the corner with its determination to drain all the mystery out of life and the universe. Everything that could be explained scientifically further diminished the realm of the spiritual.

Having retreated into a diminishing corner for several hundreds of years, the North American church culture unfortunately now reflects the materialism and secularism of the modern era. Not only do we not need God to explain the universe, **we don't need God to operate the church.** Many operate like giant machines, with church leaders serving as mechanics. God doesn't have to show up to get done what's being done. **The culture does not want the powerless God of the modern church.**

We need to take courage. Though secularism and nihilism have taken their best shot to kill God, they have lost. The postmodern world, governed by quantum physics and its emphasis on relationships, is God's end run around the modern world. A quantum world stands ready to accept divine design and divine interaction. God himself is stirring the pot. If we can pay attention we will eventually discover that not only will we not lose God in this emerging postmodern world, we will find him again!

Although the next church's shape is not yet obvious, the forces that will give it shape are. They are futures that are already present. The first of these present futures is shocking and dramatic, because it declares that much of what we call church is not going to survive.

This first new reality is in many ways foundational to the other five that follow. As with all emerging futures it presents us with a choice. It is a choice between seeking answers in pursuit of the wrong question or noodling on the tough question posed by the arrival of the new world. Its creation has made obsolete much of our goals and activities in the church world. These no-longer-relevant pursuits are reflected in the wrong question.

Wrong Question: How Do We Do Church Better?

Faced with diminishing returns on investment of money, time, and energy, church leaders have spent much of the last five decades trying to figure out how to do church better. Emphases have come and gone in rapid succession. Church and lay renewal has given way to church growth, which has given way to church health. The results beg the question.

An entire industry has been spawned to help churches do whatever it is they decide to do. Consultants, parachurch ministries, denominational headquarters, and publishing houses prod and push the church toward whatever the current fad is. A spate of program fixes have consistently overpromised and underdelivered. The suggestions are plentiful: offer small groups, contemporize your worship, market your services, focus on customer service, create a spiritual experience, become seeker-friendly, create a high-expectation member culture, purify the church from bad doctrine, return the church to the basics. After decades of this kind of environment no wonder church leaders are a little skeptical about the "next thing" and why many feel that just about the time they catch up they fall further behind. But the mailings keep coming, the seminars keep filling up, and the conference notebooks keep stacking up on the shelves.

All this activity anesthetizes the pain of loss. It offers a way to stay busy and preoccupied with methodological pursuits while not facing the hard truth: none of this seems to be making much of a difference. **Church activity is a poor substitute for genuine spiritual vitality.**

The fallout from this frenetic effort to run in place is staggering in every direction. Consider the burnout of many ministers who struggle with the increase of expectations on the part of church members. Many men and women who entered the ministry with a clear sense of call to make a difference feel overwhelmed, bewildered, defeated, and generally underprepared for the challenges they face. Having packed their bags for the journey of the church age, they now have no idea what should be in their leadership backpack for the current excursion. The portfolio of skills that once gave them standing in the community of faith no longer distinguishes them, ensures their effectiveness, or guarantees their continued leadership position. The senior pastor of a multiple-hundred-member congregation now must be manager of the corporate culture, headhunter, personnel manager, strategic planner, fundraiser, expert communicator, chief vision developer and caster, ministry entrepreneur, spiritual guru, architectural consultant, plus whatever particular assistance or role the congregation needs at any given time.

Fallout is not limited to the clergy. **Many church members feel they have been sold a bill of goods.** They were promised that if they would be a good church member, if they would discover their gifts, or join a small group, sign up for a church ministry, give to the building program, learn to clap or dance in worship, or attend this or that, they would experience a full and meaningful life. Trouble is, we don't have much evidence to support the assumption that all this church activity has produced more mature followers of Jesus. It has produced many tired, burned-out members who find that their lives mimic the lives and dilemmas of people in the culture who don't pay all the church rent.

The faithful, maybe silently or not so silently, wonder when their ticket is going to be punched, when they are going to experience the changed life they've been promised and expected to experience at church. In North America, these people have been led to believe that their Christian life is all about the church, so this failure of the church not only creates doubt about the church, it also leads them to all kinds of doubt about God and their relationship with him.

Wrong Responses

Many congregations and church leaders, faced with the collapse of the church culture, have responded by adopting a refuge mentality. This is the perspective reflected in the approach to ministry that withdraws from the culture, that builds the walls higher and thicker, that tries to hang on to what we've got, that hunkers down to wait for the storm to blow over and for things to get back to "normal" so the church can resume its previous place in the culture. Those who hold this perspective frequently lament the loss of cultural support for church values and adopt an "us-them" dichotomous view of the world. Those with a refuge mentality view the world outside the church as the enemy. Their answer is to live inside the bubble in a Christian subculture complete with its own entertainment industry. Evangelism in this worldview is about churching the unchurched, not connecting people to Jesus. It focuses on cleaning people up, changing their behavior so Christians (translation: church people) can be more comfortable around them. Refuge churches evidence enormous self-preoccupation. They deceive themselves into believing they are a potent force.

Occasionally when I do consulting for congregations I insist that the church leaders meet off-campus in a restaurant during Sunday church time. I ask the group to look around and then pose the question to them: "Do you think these people struggled with a decision this morning of whether to attend church or to go out for a sausage biscuit?" Are you kidding? The church is not even on their screen.

Some churches go to the opposite extreme. Instead of choosing refuge, their response to the collapse of the church culture is to sell out to the culture. Just today someone told me of a church billboard that promised a ten thousand dollar winner for some person who would attend and sit in the right seat! This marketing scheme is more informed by the neighboring casinos than by the New Testament. Or I think of the "worship" service of a new church I attended a few years ago on Easter Sunday. The only music that the congregation sang was the soft-rock tune, "I Can See Clearly Now the Rain Has Gone." The pastor's message addressed how to have a better marriage. Not one word about Resurrection—and this on the one Sunday of the year guaranteed to have pre-Christians in attendance! No one connected the dots for the attenders by telling them that their ultimate hope for better vision and marital intimacy is secured by divine intervention of the same God who raised Jesus from the dead. What a lost opportunity! What a pathetic and anemic response to the collapse of the church culture—a capitulation and denial of the power of the gospel. Trying so hard to be with it, this church just doesn't get it.

The point is, all the effort to fix the church misses the point. **You can build the perfect church—and they still won't come.** People are not looking for a great church. They do not wake up every day wondering what church they can make successful. The age in which institutional religion holds appeal is passing away— and in a hurry.

Before consulting one brand-new congregation, I visited their Web site. On their front page they declared that they were a church for unchurched people. Their stated vision was to "develop a congregation of over a thousand members on twenty-five acres." The people they professed to be interested in reaching could care less about how big they are or how many they are. These numbers are how church people keep score. The belief by the leadership core group was that building a better church would automatically attract seekers who were in the market for a church. They didn't understand that church hopping is for church people.

Church leaders seem unable to grasp this simple implication of the new world—people outside the church think church is for church people, not for them. We may have saturated the market of people who want to be a part of the church culture, who want church the way we do it in North America.

The pursuit of the wrong question will continue to turn the wheel of the church industry, but it will do little to expand the kingdom of God. The need of the North American church is not a methodological fix. It is much more profound. **The church needs a mission fix.**

Tough Question: How Do We Deconvert
from Churchianity to Christianity?

This tough question is about challenging the way we think about Christianity. North American Christians think in terms of its institutional expression, the church, as opposed to thinking about Christianity in terms of a movement. This shift in thinking is so profound that it resembles a deconversion, a deprogramming that we typically associate with helping people escape the clutches of a cult. Deconversion will require a disentangling, an intentional self-differentiation from church in order to gain perspective, a willingness to abandon church club member mentality for the sake of following Jesus.

In North America the invitation to become a Christian has become largely an invitation to convert to the church. The assumption is that anyone serious about being a Christian will order their lives around the church, shift their life and work rhythms around the church schedule, channel their charitable giving through the church, and serve in some church ministry; in other words, serve the church and become a fervent marketer to bring others into the church to do the same. In my denominational tradition I grew up with a telling euphemism used to describe when people became Christians: they "joined the church." The reduction of Christianity to club membership can't be said better than that.

Many church leaders confuse the downward statistics on church participation with a loss of spiritual interest in Americans. That's because these leaders can't think of Christianity outside of institutional terms. The truth is, although intrigue with institutional religion is down, interest in spirituality is up. A 2003 Gallup poll indicates that a vast majority of Americans say that religion has an impact on every area of their life. The cover of *Wired* magazine (November 2002) has a cross on it and devotes an entire section to God and spirituality. In fact, many have observed that there is a spiritual awakening occurring in America. However, it is not informed by Christian theology, and it's not happening in the church.

People may be turned off to the church, but they are not turned off to Jesus. Jesus is popular. He still makes the cover of *Time* and *Newsweek* every year (generally around Easter). As I write these lines he's just come out on the cover of a prominent scientific journal. Church people sometimes get excited by this but fail to understand that people in the nonchurch culture don't associate Jesus with the church. In their mind, the church is a club for religious people where club members can celebrate their traditions and hang out with others who share common thinking and lifestyles. They do not automatically think of the church as championing the cause of poor people or healing the sick or serving people. These are things they associate with Jesus. People outside the church see the handling of the sexual abuse scandals by the Catholic Church as an indictment on the church as a whole. They believe the church is out for itself, looking out more for the institution than for people.

A Theology of Mission

We need to recapture the mission of the church. In both Old and New Testaments we encounter a God who is on a redemptive mission in the world. In fact, we are astounded at the lengths to which God will go in pursuit of his mission to redeem the crowning achievement of his creation—people.

The central act of God in the Old Testament is the Exodus, a divine intervention into human history to liberate his people from oppression and slavery. The decisive act of the New Testament is the divine intervention of God into human history to liberate his people from oppression and slavery. In the Old Testament Moses takes on Pharaoh to liberate his fellow Israelites (though Moses is one of them, he is not one of them). In the New Testament Jesus takes on sin, death, and Satan to effect deliverance of captive kinsmen (though Jesus is one of us, he is not one of us). In both cases the deliverance is not just *from* something but *to* something. The Hebrew slaves were destined for the Promised Land, a land flowing with milk and honey. Jesus promised his followers abundant life. Included in that deal is heaven.

In both Old and New Testaments all other mini-dramas and subplots relate back to this central theme. Throughout Old Testament history God is at work on behalf of his people, whether it is raising up a shepherd boy to whip a Philistine giant or causing a pagan Persian king to repatriate the Promised Land of Palestine. In the New Testament the Spirit comes to serve as the continuing presence of God in the lives of the liberated. Much like the pillar of fire and cloud by day given to ancient wilderness-wanderers in the Exodus to guide them, the Spirit of God superintends the journey of God's people, the followers of Jesus, as they spread out from Jerusalem to Judea, Samaria, and beyond. This same Spirit would call up a man enslaved to religion and legalism and turn him into a point person in spreading the gospel of grace.

Many church leaders miss an all-important parallel in the two testaments' stories of God's interventions. God has a purpose and an assignment for the liberated people. After Moses delivered the Hebrew slaves out of Egypt, he brought them to Mt. Sinai just as Yahweh had instructed him. It was here Moses had encountered God in the burning bush and had held the conversation that launched him on his mission to Egypt. He certainly had to be curious about what was next as he climbed the mountain to be sequestered with Yahweh. He didn't have long to find out. There God revealed to Moses his heart for his people. It involved a purpose and a mission.

> Then Moses went up to God, and the Lord called to him from the mountain and said, "This is what you are to say to the house of Jacob and what you are to tell the people of Israel: 'You yourselves have seen what I did to Egypt, and how I carried you on eagles' wings, and brought you

to myself. Now if you obey me fully and keep my covenant, then out of all nations you will be my treasured possession. Although the whole earth is mine, you will be for me a kingdom of priests, and a holy nation.' These are the words you are to speak to the Israelites." (Exodus 19:3–6, New International Version [NIV]).

Yahweh rescued the Hebrews so they could partner with him in his redemptive mission in the world. They were chosen to be the priests of God, representing him to the whole earth. The significance of this designation as royal priests was not lost on those Hebrew ex-slaves. Royal priests in Pharaoh's court were very powerful figures. They were second only to Pharaoh. The Israelites' new status was quite a social promotion from their previous position as slaves. At Sinai, God delivered an assignment to his people. They were to tell the whole world about God and convince the world of his love for them. Unfortunately, Israel never quite grasped that their "chosen" status was for the sake of the mission. It incurred responsibility, not just secured the enjoyment of privileged position.

In the New Testament the apostle Peter reaches back to this episode to educate the new followers of Jesus about what it means to be in relationship with God through Jesus. "You are a chosen people, a royal priesthood, a holy nation, a people belonging to God, that you may declare the praises of him who called you out of darkness into his wonderful light" (1 Peter 2:9, NIV). Not only is the language reminiscent of Sinai and the commissioning of the people of Israel, the message is the same. The salvation secured by Jesus had come to them so they could pass it on to others. The church had inherited the purposes of God for Israel—to tell the story of the redemption as proof of God's love for all. As the priests of God's kingdom they had been given the responsibility for brokering the relationship between God and humanity.

In the book of the Revelation this special relationship between God and his people is rehearsed one final time. "To him who loves us and has freed us from our sins by his blood, and has made us to be a kingdom and priests to serve his God and Father—to him be glory and power for ever and ever!" (Rev. 1:5b-6, NIV). And in a scene in the throne room itself, those in attendance break out into song:

> You are worthy to take the scroll and to open its seals,
> because you were slain,
> and with your blood you
> purchased men for God
> from every tribe and language and
> people and nation.
> You have made them to be a kingdom
> And priests to serve our God,
> and they will reign on the earth.
>
> *Rev. 5:9–10, NIV*

Last summer the daughter of a friend of ours got married. My wife directed the wedding and decorated for it. My job was to be transportation for a bagpiper being brought in by the bride to surprise the groom (he loves bagpipes). I picked up the bagpiper from a reunion of World War II veterans. The group converges each year from all over the country to rehearse war stories and celebrate the living. They are a tight group. The reunion dynamic of war veterans who shared combat mission experience, who risked life together, who dealt with death together, is a special fellowship. This is the picture of the people of God forever united to the One with whom they have shared a life-challenging and life-transforming mission. The obvious kinship that God feels for the redeemed is tied to the special bond of being on mission together.

The North American church is suffering from severe mission amnesia. It has forgotten why it exists. The church was created to be the people of God to join him in his redemptive mission in the world. The church was never intended to exist for itself. It was and is the chosen instrument of God to expand his kingdom. The church is the bride of Christ. Its union with him is designed for reproduction, the growth of the kingdom. Jesus does not teach his disciples to pray, "Thy church come." The kingdom is the destination. In its institutional preoccupation the church has abandoned its real identity and reason for existence.

God did not give up on his mission in the Old Testament when Israel refused to partner with him. God is a reckless lover. He decided to go on with the mission himself. We do not need to be mistaken about this: if the church refuses its missional assignment, God will do it another way. The church has, and he is. God is pulling end runs around the institutional North American church to get to people in the streets. God is still inviting us to join him on mission, but it is the invitation to be part of a movement, not a religious club.

The Beginning of a Movement

When Jesus came on the scene he entered a world very similar to our own in terms of its spiritual landscape. Institutional religion had collapsed. No one really believed in the Greek or Roman pantheon of gods. People knew these beings were mere projections embodying human traits (and not just the good ones!). Judaism was also exhausted. The Sadducees (in charge of the Jerusalem Temple-based activity) had sold out to materialism and ritual. The Pharisees (holding sway in the synagogues, thereby dominating the religious agenda for most Israelites) had produced a dead religion in search of the moral high ground with God. When Jesus said, "I see dead people" (the Pharisees reminded him of tombs, Matthew 23:27 and Luke 11:44), he was not prophesying; he was stating a reality. The people of Israel in the first century knew Pharisaic Judaism had lost its luster. This is why they flocked to John the Baptist and to Jesus.

The collapse of institutional religion in the first century was accompanied by an upsurge in personal spiritual search for God and salvation. Evidence of this is seen in the two great challenges to Christianity during its early years—Gnosticism and Mithraism. In Gnosticism personal salvation was gained through possession of certain knowledge about God. In Mithraism adherents gained entrance to the cult by adopting a very strict ethical-moral code of personal conduct and then undergoing certain rites known only to the religious members (this is why this and other similar religious cults were called "mystery" religions). The emphasis in both these cases was personal salvation, not institutional development.

Jesus tapped into this widespread sentiment of disillusionment with religion but hunger for God with his teaching about the kingdom of God and how people could become a part of it. His emphasis was on universal accessibility as opposed to the exclusivity of the Pharisees. His teaching was a radical departure from the legalistic behavioral approach of Judaism. He taught and practiced grace in terms of how God deals with people. At the same time he elevated standards of personal behavior by looking past mere externals to internal heart motivations. He preached that God was *for* people, not *against* them. He defined the litmus test for genuine spirituality in terms of one's relationships—our relationships with God and with other people. He declared the first and second commandments as these: "Love the Lord your God with all your heart and with all your soul and with all your strength and with all your mind and, 'Love your neighbor as yourself'" (Luke 10:27, NIV). This emphasis by Jesus went way past the doctrinal purity standard used by the Pharisees.

The movement Jesus initiated had power because it had at its core a personal life-transforming experience. People undergoing this conversion could not keep quiet about it. They had discovered meaning for their life and wanted other people to experience the same thing. They had a much more powerful spiritual tool at their disposal than coercion or legalism. They had grace and love.

This is the dynamic of genuine Christianity. This is what turned the world upside down at the beginning of the Christian era. The time is ripe again for recapturing this initial appeal of the gospel. People are interested and searching for God and personal salvation through a relationship with him. Increasingly they are not turning to institutional religion for help with their search. In fact, just the opposite is true. They don't trust religious institutions because they see them as inherently self-serving. So they are off on their own search for God.

The current spiritual awakening in North America lacks Christian content and file systems. This is the scary part of it. Left to their own imagination people will devise all sorts of crazy stuff about God, from New Age crystals to self-enlightenment. But this is also the opportunity of the current spiritual landscape. People are open to revealed truth of God if they can get it.

Unfortunately, the North American church has lost its influence at this critical juncture. It has lost its influence because it has lost its identity. It has lost its identity because it has lost its mission.

The correct response, then, to the collapse of the church culture is not to try to become better at doing church. This only feeds the problem and hastens the church's decline through its disconnect from the larger culture. The need is not for a methodological fix. The need is for a missional fix. **The appropriate response to the emerging world is a rebooting of the mission, a radical obedience to an ancient command, a loss of self rather than self-preoccupation, concern about service and sacrifice rather than concern about style.**

The collapse of the church culture, along with the five other realities I will discuss, is God's gracious invitation to the church to rediscover itself. It will do this by dying to itself and coming alive to God's mission.

In the summer of 2002, the country spent several anxious days concerned about the fate of nine mine workers trapped in a mine in Pennsylvania. Rescue efforts involved several innovative strategies, including pumping heated air down a shaft. As the workers emerged from their ordeal, so did the story of their survival. One key element was their decision to huddle together to stay warm and in touch with one another in the cold darkness of the collapsed mine.

The church in North America far too often resembles these miners. Feeling trapped in the collapse of the church culture, club members are huddling together in the dark and praying for God to rescue them from the mess they are in. This is the refuge mentality that pervades the mentality of many congregations and church leaders. Instead, the church needs to adopt the role of the rescue workers on the surface. They refused to quit, worked 24/7, and were willing to go to plan B or whatever it took to effect a rescue.

That's the church's mission: to join God in his redemptive efforts to save the world. People all around us are in darkness. They are going to die unless someone finds a way to save them. Trouble is, the church is sleeping on the job. Too many of us have forgotten why we showed up for work.

Even worse, many of us never have known.

New Reality Number Two

The Shift from Church Growth to Kingdom Growth

The church growth movement exploded on the scene in the 1970s. It emerged from the teachings of Donald McGavran of Fuller Seminary, who brought his insights gained as a missionary to the North American church. McGavran argued that God intends his church to grow. He also asserted that the way the church was growing overseas could inform church growth efforts in America. The church growth movement was a missiological response to the initial warning signs that the church in North America had lost its mission.

Following the lead of the Charles E. Fuller Institute of Evangelism and Church Growth, church growth seminars popped up all over the country. Seminaries put church growth courses into their curriculum. Denominations trained personnel to be church growth consultants. The result is that literally thousands of church leaders have been trained or heavily influenced by the impact of the church growth movement.

Certain tenets of church growth methodology met a fair amount of resistance from church leaders. One was the principle of homogeneity espoused by McGavran, that people want to go to church with people who basically are like them. This flew in the face of the notion, still prevalent four decades ago, that America is a melting pot. Now the most prevalent view of America is

that it is a mosaic, where individual cultures maintain their identity while contributing to the overall design.

Another highly debated aspect of the church growth school
centered around the whole notion of growth. Church growth
advocates argued that growth was a sign of life and was anticipated
and even expected by God. They pointed to the teachings of Jesus
(example: the growth of the mustard seed) and the narratives of
the early church in the Book of Acts. They argued that growth
ensued when the followers of Jesus proved obedient to the Great
Commission, a command given by Jesus that has expansion and
growth at its core. Central to church growth teaching was an
admonition that church leaders should assume responsibility for
the growth of the church, and, as a corollary, if a church isn't growing it is being disobedient to God, falling short of his expectations.

Many church leaders took great exception to this approach and
emphasis on growth. They countered that growth was something
that God was responsible for. They cited instances in Scripture
where fewer was better (example: Gideon). Church growth antag-
onists lifted up remnant theology (God has a small group that
remain faithful to him) to challenge the idea that measuring the
crowd was a legitimate way of getting at true spiritual development.

The idea that the church should be growing put a lot of pressure on denominations and church leaders on whose watch the
steam had gone out of post-World War II church expansion.
After the boom of church planting that followed the migration
of the then-young GI generation from rural to urban, from urban
to suburban, the decade of the 1960s threw church leaders a curve.
The culture began a decided march away from church values, and
church leaders didn't know how to deal with a church that moved
from a privileged position to a church in exile in an increasingly
alien culture. Tending to church members who were bewildered at
the cultural shifts was draining enough, but to add pressure to grow
to the list of expectations of church leadership proved too much
for many. They felt as though they were doing well just to hang on

to what they had, especially if they were in a declining inner city or a downtown church whose members were moving further away. The sprawl of growth rings around cities created economic and social centers in communities close to where people lived and sent their kids to school. This seemed to be the place to locate growing churches. Church growth, many argued, was simply a corollary to the real estate maxim: location, location, location.

Rights and Wrong

There were a lot of things right about the church growth emphasis. It provided a wake-up call to the church, introducing a tension against the church's accepting decline as inevitable. It introduced the idea that missiological principles and practices should be applied in North America. The movement called attention to the growing diversity of the American population. It asserted cultural relevance as a key component of being obedient to the Great Commission. As a result it opened up the church to look for help in reaching the culture from sources other than church thinkers. The most notable outside resource thinkers were in the business culture. Business leaders, practitioners, and consultants provided cultural exegesis to church growth enthusiasts.

There were several things wrong with the church growth movement. A lot of "growth" was merely the migration of Christians moving from one church to another. The most notable trend was the closing down of the mom-and-pop operations and moving to the mall and, even later, to the supercenter. This was the rise of the megachurch, a phenomenon of the final third of the twentieth century. With rare exception the "growth" here was the cannibalization of the smaller membership churches by these emerging superchurches.

Church growth played to the dark side of some church leaders. The abuse of CEO privilege and position in Wall Street scandals has its counterpart in the church. The money and power that gravitate to leaders of large organizations can place extra pressures on already-cracked character foundations. Under the all-growth-is-good mantra, some unscrupulous and spiritually suspect methodologies have been employed to "get the numbers up." The rise of the celebrity-status church culture (not the child of the church growth movement, but a development of a church culture parallel to American pop culture) has created thousands of "losers," pastors and church leaders who are not serving in high-profile, high-growth churches. Consequently, a large part of the leadership of the North American church suffers from debilitation and even depression fostered by a lack of significance. The army of God has a lot of demoralized leaders.

There has been a sense over the past decade that church growth has a successor, but what is it? The most frequent nomination is some variation of "church health." Because a consensus has failed to develop on what church health is, this emphasis has failed to generate anything like the energy of the church growth movement. I think it is better to see the church health emphasis as a continuum of the church growth movement, with an expanded list of issues, including a more comprehensive look at leadership development and organizational behavior. Still, the way it is being pursued falls into two basic approaches: either it has church growth as its engine (improving church health so that the church can grow—the point still is to grow) or it is an attempt to find another way to measure success other than bottom-line numbers growth (since this is not occurring in most places).

I would argue that the church growth movement is a transition in the North American church between the old church culture and the emerging culture. It introduced a concern for growth and a missiological approach to church. Unfortunately, it fell victim to an idolatry as old as the Tower of Babel, the belief that we are the architects of the work of God. As a result **we have the best churches men can build, but are still waiting for the church that only God can get credit for.** Church leaders seem slow to grasp this. I say this because I hear the wrong question asked frequently. I am suggesting that those who are pursuing this question are in danger of more than being behind the times. They are in danger of working on the wrong building project.

Wrong Question: How Do We Grow This Church? (How Do We Get Them to Come to Us?)

One of the unfortunate side effects of the church growth movement was increased competition between congregations. Once the bottom line became the measure of success, the rush was on to acquire attendees, even if they came from other churches. In their quest to be attractive to potential congregants churches added staff, added programs, added buildings (including full health clubs), all to improve their market position. And it worked! A Lilly study released in 2002 found that one-half of churchgoers attended churches in the top 10 percent of church size. The tithe of members in these churches buys a lot more value-added experiences and services than it does in small congregations.

An entire industry of church growth experts, seminars, tape clubs, journals, and books all target church leaders who want to upfit their congregations to be competitive in the church market. Churches have jumped headlong into the customer service revolution. Many have purposefully studied the unchurched population to determine the best ways to be "seeker-sensitive" or "seeker-driven." The demand for more contemporary worship experiences required the redesign of worship services, including greater demands on worship leaders to produce high-quality musical offerings often accompanied by drama or video productions. Massive infusions of technology have been required to update member communications. Buildings have been renovated or constructed to satisfy an increasingly high-maintenance church consumer.

The church growth movement presented a steep learning curve to church leaders. Ministers who had studied theology, biblical exegesis, and other subjects in classical seminary education now signed up for marketing seminars and business courses, subscribed to the *Harvard Business Review,* and joined the American

Management Association. Seminars offered in the church world increasingly offered church growth "insights," "principles," and "prescriptions." The focus was on methodology—how to catch peoples' attention, sign 'em up, keep 'em busy, and get 'em to contribute money, talent, and energy to church efforts. There were church growth ratios to consider (how many dollars each parking place produced, how many contacts it took to close the deal on membership, how many relationships it took to "assimilate" someone, how many people could be served by a staff member, and so forth). There was human psychology to consider (what color offering envelopes helped people give more, what level of building capacity constituted "full"). There were management issues that came with the growth of staff. There was strategic planning to help break through the growth "barriers." There was the need for raising unprecedented amounts of money, requiring massive financial campaigns and a requisite growth in stewardship savvy. Communication skills had to come up to speed to connect with the informationally sophisticated audience.

Keep in mind all of this has been done with what result? Diminishing returns! I suppose you could argue that the church would have declined more significantly had all this effort not been made. That is the classic argument from silence that is hard to refute. And I don't want to denigrate these efforts. Very godly people with the best of intentions (to reach the lost) have given decades of their best energies to this pursuit. I know. I am one of those people (just take my word on my being godly).

I think it is time to wake up and smell the coffee. We can keep on this track just to watch even more dismal results (the transfer of Christians from the dinghies to the cruise ships is pretty well complete). Unfortunately, several decades of the church growth movement's emphasis on methodologies have conditioned church leaders to look for the next program, the latest "model," the latest fad in ministry programming to help "grow" the church. I am constantly asked, "what's next?" The focus of the church is on itself, on what it takes to succeed.

The target of ministry efforts of the refuge churches (who certainly have not adopted church growth methodologies) is also on the church. In these churches ministry is spent largely to provide hospice care for the dying church, to ease its pain as much as possible. The refuge churches maintain their denial through more club member activities, better club member facilities, and more staff to attend to club member needs.

More energy expended on the church's survival or success is misplaced. With the collapse of the church culture eminent, it makes little sense to continue pouring all ministry efforts on the institutional church. However, the focus of the last few decades in the church growth movement, with its addiction to methodological fixes, makes this shift almost too much for many to contemplate. To suggest some other agenda raises anxiety as well as bewilderment. That's the problem with tough questions. They are tough. And they always require a different way of thinking. People who are successful or competent in one way of thinking frequently resist a new approach. This is why revolutionaries wind up as the defenders of the status quo.

For those who are willing to take a fresh look at the demands for effective church ministry at the beginning of the third Christian millennium, a brand-new question now claims your attention.

Tough Question: How Do We Transform Our Community? (How Do We Hit the Streets with the Gospel?)

If they aren't going to come to us, then we've got to go to them. This is the crux of the issue. **Churches that understand the realities of the present future are shifting the target of ministry efforts from church activity to community transformation.** This is turning the church inside out.

Problem is, what most churches practice won't fare too well outside because they are selling membership packages (institutional wrapping: membership, fellowship, member services). The world does not want what the typical North American church has to offer. We can keep trying to get them to want what we have or we can start offering what they need. They need what people always need: God in their lives. This spiritual reality is what makes this such a tough transition. **The North American church culture is not spiritual enough to reach our culture.** In our self-absorption we don't even see the people we are supposed to be on mission to reach. Don't hear this as a call to a "deeper-life" spirituality. Often this "spirituality" is just another expression of refuge thinking (allowing Christians to hide out in Bible study). I am talking about a missional spirituality. Missional spirituality requires that God's people be captured by his heart for people, that our hearts be broken for what breaks his, that we rejoice in what brings him joy (see Luke 15).

Jesus Versus the Pharisees

Jesus faced a similar dilemma in his day. The John 4 account of his encounter with the woman at the well in Samaria has a fascinating subplot that shows how challenging it will be to reorient North American Christians. In the Sychar experience Jesus had a harder time getting through to the disciples than he did in achieving a radical life transformation of the Samaritan woman. It is possible that the disciples passed this woman on their way into town and on their way out. They apparently didn't engage her or any other Samaritan. When they returned to Jesus he was enjoying a personal spiritual experience of missional accomplishment that they were clueless about. He was so filled with joy that he had no room for food. When they wondered aloud if someone had slipped him some food, Jesus launched into a description of the smorgasbord of missional opportunity if the disciples could only learn to see. "My food," said Jesus, "is to do the will of him who sent me and to finish his work. Do you not say, 'Four months more and then the harvest'? I tell you, open your eyes and look at the fields! They are ripe for harvest" (John 4:34–35, NIV). The disciples apparently never saw the Samaritan woman. They couldn't see the harvest.

It's amazing what we don't see when we aren't looking! Learning to see from God's perspective was a teaching Jesus tried to drill home. He once told the disciples he did only what he saw his Father doing (John 5:19). At the home of Simon the Pharisee, when the woman of the street was lavishing adoring attention on Jesus, he posed the question to Simon: "Do you *see* this woman?" (Luke 7:44, emphasis added). Religious people don't see people; they see causes, behaviors, stereotypes, people "other" than them.

The reason Jesus had trouble getting his disciples to see what he saw was simply this: they had grown up in church! They had been trained to be concerned with internal issues (keeping the law, and so forth) rather than on keeping their eyes on the harvest. Not that the harvest was totally out of their mind. It could just wait (four months more) until the internal needs could be met.

The disciples had grown up under the influence of Pharisaic Judaism. **The Pharisees' evangelism strategy sounds eerily familiar.** Their approach to sharing God was, "Come and get it!" In addition, they had contorted God's message to moralism: "You people 'out there' need to straighten up!" The Pharisees had developed a very insular culture. They did business as much as possible only with other Pharisees (lest they be contaminated by the unclean). When they traveled they stayed with other Pharisees. They lived inside the Pharisee bubble (they had little Pharisee insignias on their burro bumper and listened only to Pharisee radio stations). Their message to people outside the bubble was: "Become like us (translated: believe like us, dress like us, vote like us, act like us, like what we like, don't like what we don't like). If you become like us (jump through cultural hoops and adopt ours), we will consider you for club membership." Does any of this sound familiar yet? Just hang on; we're coming to that.

Jesus' evangelism strategy directly challenged the Pharisees' approach. Instead of "Come and get it!" it was "Go get 'em!" Instead of withdrawing from people for fear of contamination, he ate with them. This was horrifying to the Pharisees. They shrieked their charge against him: "This man welcomes sinners and eats with them"

(Luke 15:2, NIV). Instead of insisting that people clean up in order to come to God, Jesus preached that God accepts people as they are so that, in the light of his love, they can come to their senses and clean up their act (the story of the Prodigal Son). Instead of advancing religious institutionalism, Jesus talked about experiencing abundant life based on personal relationship with God. He gave himself away to poor people, sick people, unclean people, the disadvantaged, and disenfranchised from the religion of the privileged. This was in direct contrast to the attitude of the Pharisees, who felt they were better than other people (remember the prayer of the Pharisee— "God, I thank you I am not like other men" (Luke 18:11, NIV).

This is why the Pharisees considered Jesus such a threat. They believed that the kingdom of God (the messianic reign) would only come on earth when enough people behaved properly (observed the law). Jesus went around telling people that the kingdom had already arrived (Luke 10:9), that it was in them (Luke 17:21). In effect, he declared that the Pharisees' ladder for success was leaned up against the wrong wall. They *had* to kill Jesus. **Religious people have always been a problem for God.**

The early Jewish followers of Jesus were steeped in Pharisee thinking. Not only did it show up in the episode with the woman at the well but also in other incidents. Consider the question put to Jesus right before the Ascension: "Lord, are you at this time going to restore the kingdom to Israel?" (Acts 1:6, NIV). Keep in mind this question was put to Jesus after Calvary, after Resurrection, after post-Resurrection appearances (walking into rooms with closed doors, and so forth), after he had served up breakfast buffets on the seashore of the Lake of Galilee. After all that, Jesus gets a question like this! "Now that we've got all this behind us, can we get back to the main point: when is the kingdom of Israel going to be restored (Pharisee nationalism)?" No wonder we have an Ascension!

The Holy Spirit also had to confront the Pharisees. Where? In the church! Jesus had predicted the course of Christianity's expansion (Acts 1:8). Under the guidance of the Spirit the movement leapt out of Jerusalem, entered Samaria through a

Pentecost-like experience (Acts 8:4–25), then jumped continents to Africa (Acts 8:26–39) and made its way into the Gentiles through the experience of Peter with the Italian soldier
Cornelius (Acts 10). Then Paul and Barnabas got the nod to be
the premier Christian missionaries (Acts 13), and the movement
touched the Asian and European continents (Acts 13–28).

Things were looking up, right? Wrong! The kingdom of God was
expanding to places, people, and cultures that Pharisees had never
considered God to be interested in. That was the problem. Reports
of all these Gentiles coming into the church raised an objection on
the part of believers who still thought like Pharisees. This thing was
out of control. They needed to get a handle on what was going
on. So they called a committee meeting to settle things down.

"Then some of the believers who belonged to the party of the
Pharisees stood up and said, 'The Gentiles must be circumcised
and required to obey the law of Moses.' The apostles and elders
met to consider this question. . . . When they finished, James
spoke up: 'Brothers, listen to me. . . . It is my judgment . . . that
we should not make it difficult for the Gentiles who are turning
to God'" (Acts 15:5–6, 13, 19, NIV).

The Pharisees were monoculturalists (all religious fanatics
are). **Monoculturalism does not embrace kingdom growth,
because it insists that people conform to a cultural standard in
order to gain admittance to the religious club.**

The bottom-line question the early church faced was this:
Will Gentiles need to become Jews first in order to receive the
gospel? We can be thankful that the leaders of the movement
answered with a resounding "no!"

Pharisees Are Alive and Well and Coming to Your Church (And They May Be You!)

Translated into our day the Acts 15 question becomes: Will people need to become like us in order to hear the gospel? Everywhere the Pharisees have influence the answer is "yes." And the

Pharisees have captured the North American church in many places. It is the expectation of Pharisees that people should adopt the church culture, including its lifestyle, if they want admittance. This is the perspective I have in mind when I refer to some church members as having a club member mentality. The assumption is that only people interested in church (the way we do it) are genuinely interested in God. This attitude is so pervasive and insidious among club members that it is rarely recognized for what it is—Phariseeism! I recently passed by a church that had a sign out on the street that proclaimed: "We do church on Sunday." I am sure that the sign committee didn't realize the real message it sent: "If you have a lifestyle that accommodates Sunday worship, then we're open for you; if not, tough."

Have you ever considered all the people we are counting on *not* to show up on Sunday at church? Medical workers, restaurant operators, utility crews, grocery store workers, gas station attendants—the list goes on and on. As Sunday restrictions on shopping and entertainment have eased, you might expect churches to be offering services for people who have to work on Sunday. Only a few do. Church leaders mostly whine about how the church is suffering under this cultural shift rather than making serious adjustments to make the church more available to people who are not a part of the church culture lifestyle anymore. A "Christian" novel I read recently had the hero of the story crusading for a return to the blue laws. The assumption of the author is that if people had Sunday's off they'd come to church. Talk about denial!

The call to take the gospel to the streets is more than the call to think up some new evangelism or outreach program. The church's efforts at these generally fall way short because the approaches are devised by a bunch of church members trying to come up with ideas that will entice unchurched people to want to come to church.

Not long ago I was invited by a pastor to spend an evening with a group he had put together that was charged with the job of developing an evangelism strategy for "outside the walls" (his phrase). My first question to them was, "How long have you been a Christian?" No one in the group of twenty had been a Christian for less than eight years. I recommended that they fire the committee! After the shock wore off, I offered an alternative to that drastic action. I suggested they recruit some unchurched people for their group, even if they had to rent them. This scenario is too typical. The assumption is that we church people know what's best for people. "Come and get it!" is our strategy, and "it" is what we have for you. We are the Pharisees.

When church people hear the tough question I am suggesting ("How do we hit the streets with the gospel?"), they still think in church terms. It goes like this: "We'll do an outreach project, but we expect that the end result is that people who choose to follow Jesus will follow him back to our church (or at least, some church)." Or I run into this attitude all the time: "We'll do this community stuff after we've handled all our internal needs, staffed all our programs, funded the services for club members, and paid salaries for ministers who spend their time almost exclusively on church members."

The target of most church ministry efforts has been on the church itself and church members. Just look at how the money is spent and what the church leadership spends time doing. We have already rehearsed the poor return on investment we are seeing for this focus.

The church that wants to partner with God on his redemptive mission in the world has a very different target: the community. In the past if a church had any resources left over after staffing Sunday School, and so on, then it went to the community. In the future the church that "gets it" will staff to and spend its resources on strategies for community transformation. Members obviously have needs for pastoral care and spiritual growth. It is critical that these be addressed. However, I am raising the question of how many church activities for the already-saved are justified when there are people who have never been touched with Jesus' love? The answer is a whole lot less than we've got going on now.

The consumer church sees resources plowed into community transformation as "diverted" from the church (read: institutional needs and programs for members). Many pastors trying to reorient church focus and resources to the needs of those outside the church run into resistance from church members who view this as a reduction of member services.

However, there are encouraging signs. Missional congregations and groups all over the country are moving this direction, following Jesus out into the streets. One congregation has launched a community ministry center called He Cares, We Care. Teams of volunteers distribute food, help people find employment, offer parenting classes. Another church turned its relocation into a community contribution. Instead of selling their old property they turned their vacated facility into a community services center. In preparation for this a church member went back to school and earned her master's degree in social work so she could serve as the center's director.

We are also witnessing the emergence of community foundations that are funded and led by people (both clergy and lay) who are attempting community transformation from a Christian perspective. They are attempting to establish a Christian presence and influence with a delivery system different from the local church's. These foundations are as different as the personality of their leaders and the charter they establish for themselves. Some resource church leaders attempt to create awareness of community needs while others target inner-city residents with issues of poverty, drug abuse, and education.

We will see more and more people, in the church and out, who have the call, the ability, and the finances to resource their own ministry passions in the community. They will not wait for the church to catch up. One clear generational distinction of the millennials (born 1983–2000) is a renewed civic consciousness. As this generational cohort matures, the Christians in it will be much more likely to volunteer and write checks for ministries' and missions' actions that make a difference in peoples' lives where they live.

Kingdom Thinking

Hitting the streets with the gospel means adopting a new way of thinking on several levels. Kingdom thinking challenges church thinking. Kingdom thinking does not force people into the church to hear about Jesus or maintain that church membership is the same thing as kingdom citizenship.

Several years ago I attended a conference of denominational executives in my own denomination. During one evening session we heard the stirring stories of a street youth ministry in San Antonio, Texas. On some Saturday afternoons a group of kids of multiethnic backgrounds, ranging in age from about nine years old to the early twenties, go into the barrios of San Antonio and put on a street concert. As people in those high-rise tenements hear the music, they inevitably come out into the streets to see what is going on. The young singers engage the people in discussion about their spiritual life and help people become followers of Jesus. The group is prepared to celebrate these life-changing decisions on the spot. Along with their sound equipment they haul in a portable baptistry filled with water. There on the streets of San Antonio they baptize people into the kingdom of God. Tears ran down my cheeks as these young people told about their experiences. It sounded like the Book of Acts to me.

Kingdom theology also will force us to reexamine our strategy for penetrating the culture with the presence of the church. **In the church age, cultural presence has largely depended on church real estate.** People had to come "inside" the church to participate in Christian worship, to observe Christian sacraments, to hear Scripture, to "join" the church. In the emerging future this "come and get it!" approach will yield to another strategy.

Jesus' strategy was to go where people were already hanging out. This is why he went to weddings, parties, and religious feast day celebrations. Jesus loved being around people who were having fun! In fact, the Pharisees accused him of being a party animal.

Let's return for a moment to Jesus' encounter with the woman at the well in John 4. How did Jesus set this up? What Jesus did was to ask for the disciples to drop him off at the well while they went on into town to pick up something to eat. Jesus knew that everyone in that town would eventually come to see him. It just so happened that the woman was his first visitor, coming in the daytime to avoid the rush hour (for reasons to do with the social stigma associated with her lifestyle).

Taking the gospel to the streets means we need church where people are already hanging out. **We need a church in every mall, every Wal-Mart supercenter, every Barnes and Noble.** McDonald's is putting most of its new stores in places where people already are—hospitals, schools, food courts, gasoline stations, Wal-Mart. I am writing these words at a Barnes and Noble bookstore. The sign on the front says they are open *every day* 9 A.M. to 11 P.M. My question is, why don't we have a church here? Short of pews, of course, couldn't we at least have someone who takes this bookstore as an outreach opportunity? Why not host a reading club for spiritual truth seekers?

I recently met with a church that is lamenting their lack of Sunday School space. Yet within two miles of this church facility are over a dozen restaurants that don't open until eleven o'clock on Sunday morning. Why not put Sunday School classes in these restaurants? If you guarantee the manager fifteen to twenty lunches, I guarantee you he'll figure out a way for this to happen. Why not offer this ministry to restaurant employees who are not going to get to any church on Sunday because of their work schedule? These Bible study groups need to be outreach oriented in order to have community impact. Otherwise we're just relocating church activity off-campus.

Just last week I was talking about this approach to a group of collegiate ministers in Texas. One guy came up to me at the break and told me that they had almost shut down their ministry center and moved everything to public settings. He had stumbled onto this strategy quite accidentally. Renovations to his building had forced his weekly Bible study to move off-site to a WhatABurger. Other students eating in the restaurant became intrigued at the group's study of Scripture and began to inquire about spiritual truth. The collegiate ministry saw more conversions at WhatABurger than any other semester when they had operated out of their student center.

By the way, I suggested going into restaurants to a minister of education of a church cramped for space. All I got back was a blank stare. When I pressed him about my idea several weeks later, he told me he couldn't figure out how it would work! His biggest issue was, in his words, "how to count it!" My hunch is he is afraid that people will like meeting at Longhorn's better than meeting at the church, and he may never "get them back" to Sunday School.

Twenty-First Century Evangelism and Apologetics

What are we so afraid of "out there?" The Pharisees were afraid of becoming contaminated, or unclean, and losing their righteousness. I think we have some different fears. I think we are afraid of not knowing how to engage people in genuine conversation. I think we fear rejection. I think we don't know what to say. I think we are unsure of what we have to offer to people. I think we are not that enthusiastic about being evangelistic because we feel we don't have a compelling story. The power of the gospel is lost on church members who can sign off on doctrinal positions but have no story of personal transformation.

Another reason we are reluctant witnesses results from our evangelism strategies. **The mental model that many church members have for doing evangelism is for them to act like telemarketers.** I mean, how popular are these people? Telemarketers interrupt you with a marketing message about a product you haven't asked for and try to get their spiel out before you hang up on them. Then, if you do happen to buy what they're selling, they pass you along to some customer service person who may or may not be actually connected to the company the telemarketer is pushing. Sound familiar yet? How many "evangelism programs" have you encountered in which sharing the gospel assumes no relationship with the customer and Jesus is sold like soap?

Let me tell you my hunch about what effective twenty-first-century evangelism will require and what the new apologetic is. I learned it from an experience my wife had a couple of years ago. Cathy went to Ground Zero in November 2001, about two months after the terrorist attacks. She traveled with a disaster relief team of people from our state denomination with a mission to clean apartments of people who had been displaced by the collapse of the World Trade Center. The apartments she cleaned had faced the Twin Towers. All the windows had been blown out when the towers collapsed. These people had watched people jump. They had found telephones, briefcases, jewelry in their apartments, all blown in when the towers came crashing down. These residents were paying commercial firms thousands of dollars to get their apartments cleaned. Our team did it for nothing, even leaving gifts behind.

At that time Ground Zero was still a police state. People could come and go only with appropriate identification. Cathy and her team had to wear their disaster relief uniforms so they could get into the area to do their work. These outfits were conspicuous and grabbed peoples' attention wherever they went. All over Manhattan people stopped them and repeatedly asked three questions: Where are you from? What are you doing? Why? Cathy tells me that by the time they answered the first two questions, "We are from South Carolina, here to clean apartments for people displaced by the terrorist attacks," they could have said anything in response to the "why" question and received a hearing. Even if people didn't understand their answer or disagreed with some point of their convictions they were willing to hear them out. Do you know why? They listened because the New Yorkers were persuaded that Cathy and her fellow cleaners believed something so strongly that it had caused them to inconvenience themselves in service to people.

This is what it's going to take to gain a hearing for the gospel in the streets of the twenty-first century—the smell of cleaning solution, dirty faces, obvious acts of servanthood. This is in sharp contrast to the image of immaculate, powerful people we Christians have typically portrayed of ourselves to the world—people in photo ops with politicians whose ear we have, people who are successful, people who are blessed materially because we are favored by God, people smug with answers. **We Christians in the church have been great about speaking the truth *without love*.** The Scriptures say we are to speak the truth *in love* (Ephesians 4:15). We *do have* the truth. The trouble is, people can't hear it from us because we haven't earned the privilege to share it.

At the point people ask us "why?" it's important to be prepared to speak the truth. To reply, "Oh, we just want to help," doesn't cut it in terms of helping people *in Jesus' name*. An insipid reply doesn't distinguish our efforts from other civic relief organizations. I was told years ago that Pastor Cho in South Korea instructs the people of his church what to say when they are asked about the intentional acts of kindness they perform (this is part of their small group evangelism strategy). When asked by those who are blessed by them why they do their kind acts, they are told to say: "I am a disciple of Jesus. I am serving him by serving you, because that's what he came to do." That response is brilliant. It sends all the right messages while avoiding a reply that creates resistance. It signals to people that God is for them, not against them, but it also provides content to what it means to be a follower of Jesus, who gave his life in service to others and invites his disciples to do the same.

I am afraid that many North American Christians, particularly evangelicals, have a very different idea of what the response should be. We feel we need to convict people of their sin and cause them to repent and change their lives. We want to tell people, "You're all screwed up. You need to clean up your act or you're going to hell." Now I don't disagree that God is in the life-changing business, nor do I diminish the issue of sin and its consequences. But our pickup lines need some serious work. I'm talking about actually gaining a hearing for the gospel in the streets instead of being flipped off.

The Challenge of Grace

If anyone had a right to confront people straight out about their wicked ways it was Jesus. He certainly didn't shy away from confronting people with the truth about their lives, but even he earns the privilege in conversation and service. Remember the episode with the woman caught in adultery (John 8:1–11)? The woman is humiliated by being brought into the circle so everyone could gawk at her. (Haven't you ever wondered where the man was who was caught with her?) She was guilty as sin (actually, guilty of sin). Caught in the very act. What is Jesus' response to this woman? First he writes in the dirt. (I think this is the only recorded time Jesus wrote anything.) In the ensuing dialogue with the crowd of would-be executioners Jesus proved that he is *for* the woman, not *against* her. He becomes her champion. (To the crowd: "You perfect people get the first pitch.") Then, after everyone is gone he tells her, in effect, "Why don't you quit living like this? It's going to kill you (it almost just did)." No shrinking back. No "I'm OK; you're OK" stuff. He forces her to confront the issue, but does it after showing his love, after championing her. The sequence is important and instructive.

Club members prefer to bullhorn people rather than engage them personally and up close. This approach fails to earn the privilege to challenge people with the truth because we haven't proved we are their champions. Instead, we have played the Pharisee role of accusing and heaping judgment. Let me say this again: people do need the truth. We do have the truth. I am talking about earning the right to share it with people who need it.

It's not our job to convict people of sin. That's the Holy Spirit's job according to Jesus ("When he comes, he will convict the world of guilt in regard to sin and righteousness and judgment. . ." John

16:8, NIV). It's our responsibility to tell good news—that God so *loved* the world that he sent Jesus.

I have a final observation about taking the gospel to the streets. It comes from debriefing my wife and daughters from an experience they had during the summer of 2002 on a mission trip to Manhattan (where Cathy had been the previous November). Their youth group was there helping to plant a church. One of the assignments the girls received was designed to help raise awareness for the new church by distributing free stuff to people on the streets and in the parks. They gave away bottled water, candy, movie tickets, and souvenir pictures of tourists they would take with Polaroid cameras and then offer the visitors. Predictably, people were suspicious of this approach. "What's the hook?" or "What's the catch?" was the question on people's mind. As a result, very few people wanted to have any conversations about the church, much less about Jesus. (As a side note, I wonder about our marketing efforts in selling the church rather than lifting up Jesus. It seems in the New Testament that Paul's strategy was to preach the gospel. He formed a church as a result of harvest. His goal was converts; the church was the natural by-product.)

Contrast this response to the girls in July 2002 to the response Cathy received just the previous November. What's the difference? Easy. And it has nothing to do with proximity to the 9/11 tragedy. The summer mission group was positioned as marketers, introducing a product with a marketing ploy similar to food vendors giving out free samples at Sam's. There was no dirt on the kids' faces. No smell of cleaning solution. No sacrifice of service.

There was one thing the mission group did that was warmly received. They set up prayer booths on the sidewalks. As people walked by they asked them if they could pray for them. Some people responded rudely, but not many. (By the way, the only people reluctant to be prayed for were "club members" who immediately replied, "I already go to church," as they kept walking.) Many people eagerly accepted the offer to be prayed for. They were not threatened by this ministry. They welcomed it. One woman burst into tears when my daughter approached her offering prayer. "My husband left me this morning and I need God's help," she said through her tears. Scores of people said, "Pray I find work." One businessman asked Cathy how long she would be around explaining; he had an important call to make in his office. Cathy initially thought his response was a brush-off until she saw him reemerge from his office building looking for her. These responses show clear evidence of the spiritual awakening that is occurring in the streets. But **since the church is absent from the streets, people are turning to all kinds of false answers to their spiritual quest. Church members then have the gall to sit inside the church and pass judgment on people for their errant beliefs!**

I mentioned earlier that sometimes we are reluctant witnesses because we don't know what to say to people. We realize that canned approaches turn people off and that many people do not accept the Bible as authoritative for them. I have a suggested strategy based on an experience I had. I was leading a conference for a small group of Christian leaders when one of the men was called out of the room. A few minutes later he returned, obviously shaken. He informed us that his father-in-law had just dropped dead of a heart attack. He told us that he had been very close to this man. Someone asked how our colleague's wife was handling the news of her father's death. "She is in shock," he said, "but she has a strong faith." The friend who had asked the question spoke up. "I don't know your wife, but the way you talked about her at dinner last night, she must be a fabulous person." This is what evangelism sounds like in conversation with pre-Christians. "I don't know this Jesus you are talking about, but the way you talk about him, he must be a great piece of work."

I reflected later on this exchange and its instructiveness for evangelism. How hard is it to talk about the people we love? When I do seminars I will frequently make this point by asking the audience at some point in the presentation what my wife's name is, how many daughters I have, and what their ages are. They never miss. And we've only been together a few hours (it probably feels a lot longer to them than it does to me)! This is why we must nurture the relationship side of our faith. Fundamentally this is what will capture the curiosity of those seeking for truth. This was the case in the first century. It is the case twenty-one centuries later.

Bottom line: we've got to take the gospel to the streets. This is the only appropriate missional response to the collapse of the church culture. I am not talking about short forays into port off of the cruise ship. I am speaking of an intentional 24/7 church presence in the community, not tied to church real estate: office buildings, malls, school campuses, sports complexes, storefronts, homes, apartment buildings, and community centers. This will be the only way we get the gospel out to people who have no intention of coming to church for their spiritual pursuits. **We need to go where people are already hanging out and be prepared to have conversations with them about the great love of our lives.** This will require our shifting our efforts from growing churches into transforming communities.

They're not coming to us. We've got to go to them.

New Reality Number Three

A New Reformation: Releasing God's People

The first Reformation was about freeing the church. The new Reformation is about freeing God's people from the church (the institution). The original Reformation decentralized the church. The new Reformation decentralizes ministry. The former Reformation occurred when clergy were no longer willing to take marching orders for their ministry from the Pope. The current Reformation finds church members no longer willing for clergy to script their personal spiritual ministry journey. The last Reformation moved the church closer to home. The new Reformation is moving the church closer to the world. The historic Reformation distinguished Christians one from the other. The current Reformation is distinguishing followers of Jesus from religious people. The European Reformation assumed the church to be a part of the cultural-political order. The Reformation currently under way does not rely on the cultural-political order to prop up the church. The initial Reformation was about church. The new Reformation is about mission.

Both Reformations have been fueled by an information revolution. The first Reformation was successful due to the breakthrough technology of the printing press. There had been plenty of localized and isolated attempts at reforming the church prior to Luther, but only with Gutenberg's invention could a sermon of grievances be distributed widely. The information revolution enabled Luther's movement to reach critical mass. The cry of the Reformation, *sola Scriptura* (Scripture as the only authority), would have meant little if people had not been able to have and to read personal copies of the Bible.

The new Reformation is also drawing energy from an information revolution. The digital revolution is producing a communication revolution that has made information ubiquitous and its access asynchronous (translation: anywhere, anytime). The result is that church members no longer have to rely on clergy for information about theology or Christian activity in the world. Nor do they have to rely on denominations to structure their giving or ministry focus. Increasingly, these are individual choices, driven by a sense of personal mission, not mere underwriting of the church or denominational program by faithful loyalists. Money is not the only resource that Christians spend. Their prayer, talent, and time are also up for grabs. The believer's mission and values are increasingly shaping the decisions on where and how these resources are distributed.

Congregations that identify with individual believers' values are the ones who stand to win. Said another way, congregations that help followers of Jesus live abundant and missional lives understand the new Reformation. Those whose message is an appeal for church members to make the church successful and significant will lose when the institutional loyalists' money runs out (by current reckoning, less than a generation away). Efforts to gain new recruits to ensure institutional support are doomed to fail. I recently passed a church sign that read, "We need one more family." Church leaders probably thought this expression would signal to passers-by that the church welcomes new people. The message being telegraphed is that the church is hungry for more resources and is desperate for another family to join and support it. People outside the church bubble are not waking up on Sunday morning hoping to find a church they can help make successful. If they do come to church, they are looking for a platform to run their lives on. They are not interested in creating institutional success.

Despite these already discernable developments in the new Reformation, most congregations go right along obsessing over the wrong question. And even for those asking the tough question, the shift is likely to be more monumental than you think. It will change how church is conceived and how it operates.

Wrong Question: How Do We Turn Members into Ministers?

Every time I see the slogan "every member a minister" I cringe. It usually means that there has been a lot of effort put into getting church members to get church work done.

One of the battle cries of the Reformation was Luther's emphasis on the doctrine of the priesthood of believers. Luther preached that all the people of God are called and gifted for service. The church got this part right. But this powerful biblical theme has been truncated in its impact, because the church has interpreted it almost solely for its own use. **This myopic vision has resulted in ministry being defined largely in church terms and lay people often being viewed as functionary resources to get church work done.** Ministers have waged an enduring campaign to convince the laity to support church efforts with energy, prayer, time, talent, and money.

Let me give you one example. In more recent decades the emphasis on spiritual gifts has often been associated with helping church members find their "ministry fit." Unfortunately, the scripting of ministry opportunities based on gift "discoveries" most usually ties back to church responsibilities. Many church members have come to see spiritual gift inventories as a recruiting tool for the nominating committee and church staff to use in "mining" church members' talent to fill church jobs.

The first two futures we have discussed have enormous implications for the role of the church member in the North American church. The collapse of the church culture and the emergence of kingdom growth as a paradigm for renewal spell the end of an era of church members playing support roles (even if those roles have been recast as "every member a minister"). Many clergy just don't get this. They view the recruitment difficulties they are experiencing as a motivational issue rather than understanding the significant shift in how people are making decisions about how they will spend their lives.

People are portfolio managers in the information age. Knowledge workers have portable skills that can be deployed in "jobs" that bring them the highest sense of satisfaction and sense of contribution. The business world is coming to understand that they don't own knowledge workers; they rent them. Knowledge workers don't work for their company. The company "works" for them, allowing them to enhance their portfolio of skills and talents. If the mission of the company fails to capture them, they are likely to move on.

This cultural development has implications for the church. **People don't want the church making decisions for them about their personal resources or mission. They don't work for the church.** This is a huge clue as to why they do not warm up to the idea of being turned into a minister (a role they see as institutional).

Turning members into ministers hasn't worked for another reason. Church members don't want to do what they see many ministers doing. On the one hand, when they see ministers being where the action is, helping people, turning lives around, partnering with God's work in the world, they line up. On the other hand, too many church members view clergy as professional ministers who have been cranked out by the church industry to manage church stuff. They have not been exposed to church leaders who are leaders of a movement. Instead, they are familiar only with institutional managers.

Most every church staff leader has been told by a layperson, "There's no way I would do what you do, putting up with the complaints of church members." What does this tell you? Many laypeople see ministers' roles as the complaint department for disgruntled club members who want to be catered to. Church members who want to live missional lives don't want to be captured by the same concerns of club members that tie up their staff ministers.

Clergy are not without culpability in this development. I see some unhealthy caregivers in ministry who are often so needy for approval themselves that they allow their boundaries to be violated by church members, then wind up bitter toward the people they are serving. They refuse to release ministry to laypeople because they would then lose their own identity. They then complain about how they are overworked, mistreated, and unappreciated. Their sense of entitlement betrays them. Some are controllers who search for status under the guise of being caring servants. Some have entered ministry largely for their own needs and then complain when those aren't being met. The point is that the current church culture has propagated a number of "ministers" who aren't very attractive to church members. This in part explains why church members don't embrace the idea of "entering ministry," whether vocationally or taking a church job.

The typical church strategy for recruiting and deploying ministry is missionally counterproductive. Frequently pastors lament to me that they can't get their high-powered laypeople "involved." They almost always think about offering them church jobs to entice them. The idea that God has gifted people only for church jobs flies in the face of his redemptive mission in the world. We ask people to leave their place of greatest connection and influence (their homes, their businesses, their schools, their communities and community organizations) to come to the church to do some church work! Many church members have large life and work agendas. Sitting in church pews are people who lead multibillion-dollar multinational corporations, own their own businesses, work with dozens of school students, serve in governmental and political agencies—the list goes on and on. Why should they leave these to tend to matters that can easily be handled by those who enjoy the church scene? I am not saying that ushering or serving on the finance committee are unimportant.

It's just that limiting church member contributions to these responsibilities reflects a lack of missional awareness.

Laypeople see the disconnect in the "every member a minister" strategy. They are voting by not lending their time, energy, and money to ministry "vision" that has the church as the primary beneficiary or recipient. Church has become increasingly irrelevant to their workaday and home lives. Church ministry to them is an add-on activity to an already crowded life. They wonder why God can't use them where he has already embedded them—in their homes, workplaces, schools, and communities.

We have failed to call people out to their true potential as God's priests *in the world.* If we are going to correct this we are going to have to pursue a quest different from turning members into ministers.

Tough Question: How Do We Turn Members into Missionaries?

The subtext to this question is: How do we deploy more missionaries into community transformation? This will require that we not only release ministry but that we also release church members.

If you are a church leader, be aware that when you head down this road toward developing a missionary force, you are going to do some significant soul-searching and ministry reprioritization. Your church budget may shrink. Your church calendar may get less crowded. You may not have as many meetings. You will lose control of the church ministry. You are going to be challenged not only to release ministry, you are also going to be challenged to release members from churchianity, to quit gauging their spiritual maturity by how much they "support the church." You may see them less, but you will exponentially increase your impact on their lives and your impact on the community where your church is located.

If you think this isn't hard, then think again. I spent three days a few years ago with a group of senior pastors of large megachurches. These congregations are successful by current standards of gauging church success. Their memberships are large and growing. Their ministry programs are vibrant. The pastors were convened around the topic of leadership development. Early on in the session I suggested that we talk about an agenda for community transformation. They looked at me with blank stares. Then one spoke for the group, politely dismissing the suggestion as something they would talk about later after they worked on what they perceived to be their greatest leadership development needs. For two more days they wrangled over the best way to devise lay ministry processes to produce enough leaders in their congregations to get church work done. At the end of our time together they had given not even five minutes of attention to an agenda that reached beyond their church program and real estate needs.

This is what life in the church bubble can do to you. It shrink-wraps your vision down to the size of your church. It convinces leaders that people are paying rent for the rest of their lives just so they can do church work. I understand this dynamic. I still remember the shock a decade ago when I moved from local congregational ministry and discovered there was life beyond church. I suddenly understood the challenges laypeople face in adding church responsibilities to everything else. I also became suddenly aware of the sacrifices the leaders had made in the church I had pastored. I was grateful that our work together had been very missional and worthwhile, but I respected their contribution even more when my lifestyle came to resemble theirs.

What are some implications or some issues you must tackle in pursuit of the tough question of reimagining and reengineering your church from ministry sponge into a missionary sending agency? Here are some suggestions.

The Need for Missiology

A few years ago I visited the Polynesian Cultural Center on Oahu in Hawaii. My family and I spent an entire day there enjoying the shows, the food, and the archeological and historical exhibits of the various Polynesian cultures. The center is owned and operated by the Mormon Church. When I left the complex we headed back toward Honolulu on the King Kamehameha Highway. Several miles down the road I passed a sign on the side of the road that simply read: Baptist Church. An arrow underneath the words indicated that we needed to take a right turn down a small road to get to the church. As I passed that sign it struck me that I had just seen the difference in approach between people who think like missionaries and people who think like club members. Mormons have incorporated a missionary perspective into their spiritual formation process. When they moved into the South Pacific they began to study and celebrate the culture. They are now the fastest growing spiritual group in Hawaii. The Baptist congregation who put up the sign on the road was advertising to people who were like them already. "All you Baptists who washed up on the island, our club meeting house is right down this road." Hardly a missionary mentality!

Over the past several decades the North American church has focused on a number of theological issues, depending on the challenge perceived by the church. The Pentecostal movement forced the issue of pneumatology—doctrine of the spirit, specifically the study of spiritual gifts—to the forefront as church leaders grappled with various charismatic issues, especially the theology of gifts. The praise and worship movement caused the theology of worship to receive needed attention. Some denominations fought wars over the doctrine of revelation, particularly as it relates to the authority of Scripture. A growing religious pluralism will cause us to visit various articles of the faith in the future, especially the doctrines of soteriology (the issues of sin and salvation) and Christology (the person of Jesus). The church must always be visiting and revisiting theological issues.

I am proposing that missiology come into prominence, both as a theological pursuit and as a guiding operational paradigm. Even the issues that have captured the church's attention should be framed against the backdrop or under the overarching theme of missiology. For instance, the discussion of worship unfortunately often occurs without a missiological perspective. Witness the church worship wars. These are the result of club members discussing their worship style preferences as stockholders and stakeholders, not as missionaries. The usual goal is to find something that club members like. We've all heard discussions among church leaders involving questions such as, "Can nonbelievers really worship God?" or "Should our worship be seeker-sensitive or seeker-driven?" as though worship is not a powerful evangelistic tool to express the church's mission in the world! Nonbelievers are already worshiping, because people are built to worship something. Our challenge is to upgrade their worship to worship of the true God. The point is, absent a missiological center, North American theological reflections can easily drift toward figuring out who's right and who's wrong rather than who's going with the gospel, who's listening, and who's responding.

The need for missiology can be argued from pure demographics. North America is the largest English-speaking mission field in the world. It is the fifth or sixth largest mission field of any stripe. If we are not focusing on missiology, we are being disobedient to the Great Commission.

Missiologists do cultural exegesis. Missionaries understand that being culturally relevant is critical to an evangelism strategy. However, many church leaders in North America who attempt to connect with the culture are pilloried for their efforts and looked at as having abandoned the faith. Of course, where does this criticism come from? The church crowd. **Only people without a missiology disdain attempts at being culturally relevant.**

The point is not to adopt the culture and lose the message; the point is to understand the culture so we can build bridges to it for the sake of gaining a hearing for the gospel of Jesus. Some years ago I was called by a church leader who asked me if I would supervise his Doctor of Ministry project. When I asked him what he proposed to study he put it like this, "I want to do a worship project that examines how far we can go in being culturally relevant and still remain faithful to the Great Commission." I told him that was the wrong question. "You cannot be faithful to the Great Commission *without* being culturally relevant," I said. Then I asked him, "What do you want to be—culturally irrelevant?" He never called back.

Let's talk a minute about what it means to do cultural exegesis. For starters, it means we need to go to language school. That's what missionaries do who are interested in reaching a culture with the good news of God's saving work in Jesus. I'm talking about more than checking our church talk against street understanding (for instance, "lost" doesn't communicate, nor does "saved" or "inviting Jesus into your heart" or "repent" or "the world" or a whole host of other terms that church members use in church-speak). The issue, I fear, is not about our ability to do this; it's about pride and our lack of concern for people God is concerned about. We don't want to give up "our" culture or "our" language for others' sake. **This reluctance to connect with people outside the church is just further evidence that the church culture in North America is a cultural phenomenon in America that is more about a particular religious culture than about Jesus or his mission.**

When people hear me talk about learning the language of people outside the church, they sometimes resist on the basis that this is pandering to the culture. How absurd! We don't think that missionaries to Russia during the cold war became Communists when learning Russian. Nor are we worried that missionaries learning a tribal dialect of an unevangelized group means they will adopt a pagan lifestyle. I am amazed at how many congregations will cheer denominationally produced videos of foreign mission efforts that include contextualized worship experiences (native dance, native instruments) but, when the lights come on, rant against the same strategy in their clubhouse. This shows up dramatically in the worship wars. Missiologists know that people must worship God in their own heart language. North American church club members are quite willing to deny this privilege even to our own church kids in order to preserve the club culture.

The call for us to go to language school really is larger than a call to vocabulary review. It is a call to study the cultures in North America. Of course this is important for reaching ethnic groups. But this is also important for understanding the broadband English-speaking culture in North America. A continuing failure to engage the culture will doom the church into a death spiral as the members of the church culture die off in the next twenty to thirty years.

A missiological approach to the emerging world will take into account the largest cultural shift under way and its implications for the church. It is the transition from the modern to the post-modern world.

The Modern World

The world that has been dubbed the "modern" world came into existence roughly five hundred years ago. It emerged as a result of the confluence of several new technologies, notably a break-through in shipbuilding that produced the caravels (ocean-worthy vessels capable of circumnavigation of the globe) and the invention of the printing press. These technological advances, combined with a shift in philosophy, gave rise to the "modern" mind. Newton and Descartes gave us the scientific method and a rationalistic view of the universe. This shift was trumpeted as the liberation of humankind from the "Dark Ages" into an Age of Enlightenment. Aristotelian materialism gained ascendancy over Plato's metaphysics. Moderns asserted it was time for humanity to move past superstitions and musings about unseen worlds and forces previously uncomprehended. What was real was what could be observed (seen, touched, and counted), and if it could be observed it could be explained.

The modern world was bent on demystifying everything. Modernity vigorously studied the universe to wring from it its secrets and expose its inner mechanisms. This gnosis was accomplished by tearing things apart to get at their meaning: "If we can understand the parts, we can understand the whole." Human reason was exalted. Education became the religion of the world. The map became shaped by a new political order, the nation-state, which gave rise to economies and militaries that have shaped the geopolitical history of the last five centuries.

God took a beating in the modern world. From beginning to end the modern world has challenged the idea of God and what his role in the universe really is. The modern minds' enthusiasm for science and technology seemed bent on putting God in his place, but that place was hugely diminished, considered to be beyond the realm of the "verifiable" and irrelevant to the "real" world. Throughout the modern centuries God has been systematically taken out of circulation and increasingly relegated to religious ceremony. The Founding Fathers, for instance, who crafted the nonestablishment clause in the Bill of Rights, would be dumbfounded to discover that two and a quarter centuries later this could and would be interpreted as a separation of God and state.

The church inevitably changed in response to the modern world. The Reformation, the spiritual counterpart to the Enlightenment, shifted the basis for leadership. No longer would church leaders hold their position based on their knowledge of spiritual rites and otherworldly things. The Reformation requalified the pastor as a leader by virtue of education, particularly as a scholar of antiquities (Hebrew and Greek texts). Five centuries later the pastor would gain and maintain leadership of large superchurches through a grasp of organizational science and would feel quite at home in business conferences with CEOs and senior management types. This migration of church leadership precisely tracks with the economic development of the modern world that has given rise to bureaucracy and organizations and management.

The church in North America is thoroughly modern. It has reduced its understanding of spirituality to numbers that can be reported (the triumph of materialism over spirit). A church is doing well if membership, giving, and facility square footage are all increasing. The church is print reliant. The Bible has become for the modern church the supreme manifestation of the Word of

God (not Christ) because it is "objective" truth (a modern distinction). It became the fourth member of the Trinity. The sermon (an explanation of text) has replaced the mass (along with the mystery of God's intervention). Preaching reflects the Newtonian world, approaching the text as a body to be dissected into shreds of words and even parts of words (called exegesis).

The approach to spirituality in the modern church has been to adopt the world's educational model. Sunday "School" reflects the basic assumption that the path to Christian maturity involves the acquisition of biblical information. (This assumption means that there were very few growing Christians before people could carry leather-bound, codex versions of the Scriptures. Of course, they couldn't have read them even if they had had them.) Graduation from confirmation classes in many church traditions largely has to do with the ability to sign off on certain doctrinal positions. If you can pass the test, you're in. The modern approach to spirituality adopts Kantian metaphysics. We focus on the Bible because the thing-in-itself (God) is really beyond us. Contrast this to the quest of medieval mystics who sought and attained personal intimacy with God. In a premodern (and postmodern) world there was not the interposition of text between soul and God, nor did spiritual maturity rely so much on human reason's ability to grasp, understand, and explain.

The result of the modern church's form of spirituality is a North American church that is largely on a head trip. This is at the heart of why the lifestyles and values of people in the church mirror so closely the lifestyles and values of people in the larger culture. We have a rational faith. The test for orthodoxy typically focuses on doctrinal stances, not character and spiritual connectedness to God and others. Faith, in the modern world, is about intellectual assent, not belief in the biblical sense.

In keeping with modernism, Christians in North America practice their faith in a segmented approach, separated from other parts of life (business, family, and so forth). This is why we go to "church" to do our spiritual activity. This is why we don't do spiritual formation at home—that's what the church is for. After all, spiritual "education" should be left to the professionals who have the training and credentials for it. The end result is parents unable to talk to their kids about God, church members who take their teenagers to church (believing that this activity inoculates them against the influence of a pagan culture) but don't talk about life implications of faith, couples who are embarrassed to pray together—the list goes on and on.

At the advent of the modern world the church was frantic in its questioning, "Where is God?" in a universe suddenly shown not to be fixed, not to revolve around the earth, not tied to an unmoved Mover. Initially the church responded by declaring astronomical discoveries to be heresies. "Where is God?" is again the fearful cry of Christians who are afraid of losing God in the new, emerging world. Because the church clings to the modern world, we now have a church in North America that is more secular than the culture.

The Postmodern World

An honest search for God today would lead the church back into the world, because postmodernism is at heart a spiritual movement (don't hear "Christian" movement). It is a search for meaning. It is the alternative to the nihilism that so many people predicted to be the next phase of Western thought. Postmodernism refuses to be forced into the synthesis of the Hegelian dialectic. It allows for ambiguity; it countenances opposing notions at the same time (quantum physics, foundational to the postmodern world, asserts that light is both a particle and a wave); it intensely refuses a sacred-secular dichotomous view of life. Everything is sacred; nothing is sacred—both are expressed in postmodern thought.

At its heart the emerging postmodern worldview supports two seemingly contradictory notions about the way the world works. The first is the power of one. In the modern world nations fought wars against nations. As I write these lines the only superpower in the world has been for over a year searching for one person, Osama bin Laden, who has declared war on the United States, and we are at war against another person, Saddam Hussein. A few years ago one teenager in the Philippines launched a computer virus (remember "I love you"?) that had global impact and cost more to clean up than the GDP of many countries. The Army recruits with the slogan "An Army of One," which is strange to modern thinking, because an army by definition is a group.

This last notion introduces the other major tenet of postmodern thought—that we are all connected, that no one is isolated. The digital revolution and computers have made individuals both independently powerful and amazingly connected at the same time. What once required a team of office workers to produce is now accomplished on a single PC. The entire world can be touched by a few keystrokes. Where you are doesn't matter as long as you have "access" to the Internet, the global platform of connectedness.

The science of quantum physics also contributes to this new way of thinking. The quantum universe is not a universe of things but a universe of relationships. The modern mind viewed the universe as a giant machine that could be explained if you could strip it down to its component parts. The quantum vision of the universe is more interested in the whole, in how things interrelate. Its fundamental unit is not even single, but plural. The subatomic world comprises quarks in relationship to other quarks (they do not exist outside of community). The quantum universe is a created universe, a giant thought, not the giant thing of modernism. It evidences design and intentionality, not randomness and natural selection. **Room for God is growing in the postmodern world.** The number of scientists who believe in creationism is on the rise.

Postmoderns are wildly spiritual. It is a spiritualism that reflects a hunger for meaning and connectedness. It is a spiritualism that seeks to unite people of faith (a shift from the modern era's fracturing and splintering into denominations, sects, and so on). It is a spiritualism that starts with an affirmation of the basic goodness of humanity (in direct contrast to the "depravity of man" doctrine in Protestantism). Redemption in postmodernism is about loving others and serving others (Hard Rock Café: love all, serve all). Righteousness is not a coming to terms with a perfect God who is concerned about a moral code. It is about getting relationships right with other people. A relationship with God is assumed (a real challenge to evangelism strategies that rely on convincing people they are separated from God in order to begin a conversation). The cross is a symbol of brokenness. Brokenness is what unites people in the postmodern world. It is the common ground. The postmodern definition of sin is stunted life and stunted potential, a sense of corporate guilt that the world is not the loving place it should be.

Heaven and hell are here and now in postmodern thought. Life goes on beyond this worldly existence, though what it will be is fairly ill defined. It will be better, and it is a life of connectedness with loved ones. Miracles are expected and common (a direct opposite view of modernity). There are no coincidences. Everything is purposefully connected, and this connectivity itself is proof of a loving God who wants people to love each other. However, there is little tolerance for institutional-brand religion that focuses more on its own support and survival than on helping people.

Believe it or not there are people who believe that the entire postmodern "thing" is not real or is merely a passing fad. One asked me just this week, "Are things really changing this much or are these things you are talking about just Reggieisms?" Then there is the pastor who told me, "I don't believe in that stuff," as if we were discussing ghosts, UFOs, and alien abductions. He is a pastor who typifies deep denial in the church and the fear that keeps people locked in that dungeon. He continues to operate his church for traditional club members (he resists all forms of contemporary worship), hoping that he will be the hot church in town when the culture swings back his way. He presides over fewer and fewer people who are just like him. In a strange psychological twist, this further confirms his views that he is a part of the faithful remnant.

There are other reasons that postmodernism is pooh-poohed. Recently a student in one of my classes voiced the opinion that postmodernism is really just the last gasp of modernism and not really the new world yet. Frankly he and I will both be long gone before we know whether he's right or not. You may not like the term; you may wish it weren't so; you may not know exactly how to classify it, but you know things are vastly different than they used to be, and there seems no end in sight to the changes that are altering the culture year by year and leaving many of us bewildered. (Just this morning a group has claimed to have produced the first human clone.)

Enter the Church?

These developments are part of the reason I say **we have a church in North America that is more secular than the culture.** Just when the church adopted a business model, the culture went looking for God. Just when the church embraced strategic planning (linear and Newtonian), the universe shifted to preparedness (loopy and quantum). Just when the church began building recreation centers, the culture began a search for sacred space. Church people still think that secularism holds sway and that people outside the church have trouble connecting to God. The problem is that when people come to church, expecting to find God, they often encounter a religious club holding a meeting where God is conspicuously absent. It may feel like a self-help seminar or even a political rally. But if pre-Christians came expecting to find God—sorry! They may experience more spiritual energy at a U2 concert or listening to a Creed CD.

A church paying attention to the culture would realize how ripe the times are for a genuine Christian movement in North

America. A culture desperate for God comes to church after every single major crisis, whether it's a local school shooting or the national 9/11 event. They are in search of sacred space and sacred connections. And increasingly, they are creating their own, whether in neighborhood cul-de-sac candlelight vigils or a Ground Zero shrine, complete with towers of light beaming heavenward as symbols of hope.

I think a lot of church leaders and church members are intimidated by all the God-interest in the culture at large. I think we don't know how to hold conversations about God. We've only been taught to sell our brand of religion. We are so intent on convincing people that their life is screwed up, their faith is wrong, their beliefs messed up, and so forth, that we are inept at listening and engaging people. We look at people as "prospects" for membership (this term is actually still used) rather than as spiritual beings with the same quest for God. We have failed at missiology. We don't know how to function in a culture of religious pluralism. We own God, and others have no right to him except on our terms.

For centuries our approach has been to try to hold on to God in a scientific, technological, mechanistic universe intent on destroying him. To survive in that environment we have unwittingly adopted that modern mind-set. We can argue for the existence of God and can argue for the veracity of Scripture and can present "proofs" of the Resurrection. But it's cold. It's mental. It's passionless. Now the world doesn't demand what we offer anymore. **In fact, many people outside of the church are more spiritually passionate and enthusiastic about God than many church members.** They no longer need our kind of convincing.

Herein lies the other intimidating factor about this new spiritual awakening that is under way in the culture. We are afraid deep down that we don't really offer a viable experiential alternative to the spiritualism that is so patently powerful in the lives of many outside the church. We are afraid of being shown up as spiritually deficient. So we retreat to familiar bastions of taking moral stands and railing at the inadequacies of other faith systems. Again, poor missiology. But it reflects the attitude of a people who think they are in danger, so they defend their power and position against challengers. Too bad we don't just realize we are no longer in charge spiritually and we are going to have to engage the culture in order to get a hearing for the gospel of Jesus.

Paul, the premier Christian missionary, can teach us how to be missionaries in a culture that closely resembles his in terms of spiritual landscape (religious pluralism, collapse of institutional religion, heightened search for spirituality). Early on, in Athens, he took on other religions at the Acropolis to point out the superiority of Christianity in a religiously plural marketplace. Even though he argued eloquently at Mars Hill, he had very little luck in his approach. It seems that he learned from this experience that it was not superior reasoning but superior living and superior loving that was the best approach to engaging the culture with the attractiveness of the gospel. This is why the apostle focused so much on righteous living, not because of a Pharisaical, legalistic bent but out of a missiological conviction.

Paul came to understand that a vibrant relationship with Jesus would be an attractive way to live and would intrigue people about how they could get hold of the same kind of life. This is precisely how he catalogs his spiritual journey in Philippians 3— a journey from a legalistic zealot for God to having an intimate relationship with him.

A Missionary Movement

Don't plan on taking a vote on whether your church will release members to become missionaries. What you must do is two things: create a culture informed by missiology and create venues where people can practice being missionaries.

Creating an informed missiological culture can be done in a number of ways. Here are a few suggestions.

Discuss Generational Cultures. You can begin cultural exegesis inside your own congregation. Those of us in the church industry may be aware of generational cultures, but many of us aren't educating our congregations about it. Every time I do the simplest, broad-brush painting of generational differences (including values, heart language, work preferences), people respond with great interest. Some even seem relieved (especially older people who think their kids and grandkids are a little bit weird). Trust me, they don't know this stuff. They aren't hearing it anywhere. I remember talking with a seminary board of trustees about gen Xers. When I finished, a board member introduced himself to me as the owner of nineteen fast-food restaurants. "You just told me why I can't keep my gen X managers." An exegesis of generational cultures will help people not only at church, but also at work and at home.

Discuss the Emerging Culture. You might want to bring in people from the outside to do this. Maybe you feel uncomfortable doing this, or you may not feel qualified. Find a person who is not a church person to come in and inform the congregation on what people outside the church bubble need and what people think. This is a big reverse, letting pagans testify to believers (unless you are afraid some of the church members will convert!).

Explore Community Needs. This can be done in a variety of ways. You can access psychographic information from demographic services. You can invite community leaders in for forums. You can send people out with questions, for instance: What do you think are the one or two most critical needs in our community? Notice this is different than asking people what they would like to see in a church. Remember, they may not be interested in making you successful, but they might be interested in you if you want to improve their lives and your community.

Expose Yourself to a Missionary Church. First, go see them. Shoot some video. Bring some leaders from the missional congregation to talk with your leaders. Pick up ideas and share them. Second, create venues for missionary service. People who want to be a part of a missionary force may still need ideas about ways they can give expression to their passion to touch the community.

Build for the Community. Some churches do not build buildings for themselves. They build buildings for community needs, open them to the community, and use them for church functions. One congregation is currently exploring a partnership with the YMCA by providing land for a Y facility in exchange for the privilege of conducting Bible study classes there on Sunday and during the week.

Adopt a School. One church in West Virginia adopted a nearby elementary school. The congregation was exclusively senior adult, but the members began literacy classes, math tutoring, and other learning activities after school (at the school). As a result several families with children were reached with the gospel. Some even came to their church.

Pay It Back. A congregation in New Jersey celebrated its twentieth anniversary with the inauguration of a campaign to invest in the community as a payback for community support throughout the years. Called "Give It Back," the emphasis will involve helping people with job placement, car repairs, furniture distribution, food, financial help, and financial planning. Another church is planning to follow up its current building campaign with a fundraising campaign to raise several million dollars for community needs and services.

Get Out There. Many churches are beginning to insist that each Sunday School class or small group should have a local missions project. One California church bought an old theater complex and actually runs family movies to give families an entertainment option. A church in the Pacific Northwest holds its summer services all outdoors in the park. A church on the South Carolina coast always baptizes in the ocean on a public beach as witness. A youth ministry not far from where I live has renovated a restaurant for an after-school hangout. One five-year-old specializes in community programs, not church activities, and has organized community soccer, football, and baseball leagues. A man in my neighborhood leads a men's group every Saturday morning in his home. Some guys have become Christians because of Mike's ministry. A couple near Charlotte has addressed their burden for gen Xers by starting a discovery group at their home, because few of this generation are coming to their church.

Go First. If you are a pastor or staff member of a local congregation, you must model missionary behavior for the church to see. One young pastor is formally asking his church to release him to the community for two days per week as a missionary. His situation is like tens of thousands of others around the country. The neighborhood where his church is located has shifted over the years. No one from the community right around the church attends. The church does not want to relocate, but neither does it intentionally reach out to the people across the street from the front, side, or back doors. This pastor, through his request, is sending all the right messages. And by the way, he is asking for permission to actively recruit church members to help him with ministry needs and opportunities as they are uncovered.

If you are a lay leader, you don't have to be cut out of the action. You might want to lead your church Bible study, your care group, or your ministry team to develop some community ministry. This might involve moving off campus. It might precipitate a complete shift in your ministry focus as you contemplate your missionary strategy. Your ministry efforts might find more expression outside the church than inside.

Don't wait for everyone in the church to catch up to where you are. **You go first. Others will follow.**

These ministry efforts are not add-on things to do but are part of a community orientation that is fundamental to the church's mission. **Releasing people to be missionaries will turn your congregation inside out.** It will help people and families integrate their lives around their sense of mission by reducing the compartmentalization that plagues them. Rather than trying to attract people's leftover energies (after work, school, family, and so on), release them to find and give expression to their missionary calling. Then watch the energy flow! The key is to have a practice of saying "yes" to people's ideas about ways to be on mission.

Warning! Warning!

This new Reformation, turning members into missionaries, will precipitate a crisis, both in individuals and in a congregation. Member values clash with missionary values. Member values are all about church real estate, church programming, who's in and who's out, member services, member issues (translated: am I getting what I want out of this church?). Missionary values are about the street, people's needs, breaking down barriers, community issues (translated: am I partnering with God's work in people?).

One of these value sets will triumph over the other. They do not coexist peacefully. Anyone who has tried to lead a church transition from club to missional congregation can tell you this. They can show you their stigmata received at the hands of club members. Resistance to missionary values often occurs even in churches that are reaching people. The reason is simple. If their growth is occurring because they offer the best church game in town, club member values usually predominate. Just start talking about reducing time at church so church members can have more time to invest in the community and see how warmly received that suggestion is. Club members are clueless about developing relationships outside the club. Just begin offering tickets to the

Christmas pageant only to members who bring pre-Christians. A howl will go up from the crowd who demand holiday entertainment. Start simplifying the church calendar by reducing the number of activities for club members. Start doing more away from the church. Start partnering with other believers from other churches to establish community ministry initiatives. You will find out how entrenched and how entitled club member values are.

Persecution of church leaders in the North American context does not come from outside the church. It comes from inside the church. I have never had a church leader say to me, "I am quitting. The pagans are getting to me!" I've had dozens of them say, "I can't take the club members anymore."

Church members trying to be missionaries are not immune from persecution either. I know people who have given up church responsibilities to create more time in their schedule to minister to people outside the church. Sometimes their reward has been to receive much less warm greetings from staff members who tried to recruit them for church jobs and were turned down. Some have been tagged as "unfaithful" to the church or "not committed." What a sad day when answering the call to live on mission earns you the ridicule of the church.

If club member values weren't so well ensconced, churches would be strategizing more about intersecting with people away from church. I am writing these lines on a Sunday evening in a bookstore, sitting across a study table from my college freshman daughter. She attended church this morning at a church that has started adjacent to the campus where she lives. Somebody had the vision to start a church in the college students' world. Several hundred other churches in the area claim to have a college ministry, but they are hoping they can attract students to leave the campus on a Sunday morning to go to church. My daughter said, "It was so cool just to walk a couple of blocks to church."

OK, so maybe establishing a church is too ambitious for these other local churches, but how about sponsoring some spiritual activities on campus (a Bible study, worship, for example)? I talked to a college minister this past week about doing this. His response was that the senior pastor of his church wanted to see these college kids at church. "That's all that counts," this college minister told me. "I could have hundreds involved on the campus, but only the ones who show up at church count in the numbers I am responsible for generating." Talk about club values! Where do you think this college minister has his office? At the church! That makes good sense for a staff geared for club member services but no sense at all in a missionary culture.

Changing the Scorecard

Adopting a missionary approach will require changing the scorecard. Church scorecards currently reflect member values: how many show up, pay up, and participate in club member activities. These are the numbers used to compare one church with another—the numbers that denominations ask for in their reports. These numbers establish the pecking order among clergy. The bigger the better and the more respected by club members of other churches.

A missionary church culture will need to begin keeping score on things different from what we measure now. These may include how many ministry initiatives we are establishing in the streets, how many conversations we are having with pre-Christians, how many volunteers we are releasing into local and global mission projects aimed at community transformation, how many congregations are starting to reach different populations, how many congregations use our facilities, how many languages (ethnic and generational) we worship in, how many community groups use our facilities, how many church activities target people who aren't here yet, how many hours per week members spend in ministry where they work, go to school, and get mail.

Until we start making heroes of people who decide to be and act like missionaries, we will fail to turn club members into missionaries. Until we bless people who "go out" from us to reach people who may not come to us, we will continue to have a king-dom vision that is shrink-wrapped to church programs and church real estate. Until we start adopting schools and hosting commu-nity food banks and teaching parenting seminars and holding financial planning seminars for the people who come to us for food, we will keep fostering club member mentality.

I had just spoken to a group of church leaders in a small town. Representatives of three different churches were present. I pleaded with them to consider doing less church stuff and doing more ministry aimed at the pre-Christian culture. When I finished speaking, a man approached me and introduced himself to me as a deacon in his church. He said, "From now on, when some idea comes up for something new to do at our church, I am going to ask the question, Who is this for?"

Who is this for? may be a good way for you to begin your own journey from member to missionary. Think about your life, your money, your time, your talent, and your commitments. *Who is this for?* Is the answer club members or people who do not yet know Jesus?

God help you to be a missionary. God help you release mis-sionaries into the world with the gospel.

New Reality Number Four
The Return to Spiritual Formation

He approached me at the end of the conference I was leading. "I teach the new Christian class," he said. "I'm just surprised. You know, they don't know anything." He went on, shaking his head. "They don't know anything about the Bible, about God, about sharing their testimony, or about the church."

His remarks typify club member attitudes: "We don't do diapers." Club members want people coming into the church and into the faith fully grown and church trained.

He pressed me, "What do you think I ought to teach them?" I could tell the question was a prelude to a demonstration. "What are you teaching them?" I asked. "I've put together a notebook," he said as he pulled out his exhibit. It would have taken two llamas to carry that thing.

I drew a deep mental breath and plunged in. "I bet there's a lot of good stuff in there," I said. "You might consider another approach. If I were responsible for coaching a group of brand-new Christians, I think I would conduct the group like a marriage enrichment seminar. These people have just gotten married to Jesus. They have fallen in love with him and have just committed themselves to him for life. How do we help them keep their relationship growing?" To drive the point home I added, "I'm so glad that my wife did not turn to me on the way to our honeymoon and say, 'Now that we've gotten the wedding ceremony behind us, I've taken the liberty of putting together a notebook. . . .'" I don't think he bought the approach or saw the humor.

Christians (evangelicals especially) emphasize that our connectivity to God is through a relationship with Jesus. We talk about giving him our hearts or inviting him into our hearts. We use love language to talk about committing our lives to him. Then, as soon as the deal is done, we switch the language and go to head stuff. We pull out the notebooks. We go over what we believe, information about the church, and so on.

I have learned a few things about Cathy in our two-plus decades of marriage. I have discovered what she likes and doesn't like. I have learned about her family. I don't know *about* her. I know *her!* (She just called while I was writing. From her first word I knew her mood, not from her words, but from her tone.) She and I have achieved an intimacy that comes from hanging out together, sharing dreams and hurts, working on projects together (like raising two daughters, pastoring and leading a new church, redecorating rooms—she's an interior design consultant), experiencing leisure and fun together, and from sharing countless days of more routine experiences. I can finish some of her sentences. I know what she thinks about a lot of things now without having to ask anymore. We have had both romantic moments and contentious arguments. Even while we've been developing as individuals our growth has been bent toward each other, like plants searching for sunlight will bend toward it. This is how a relationship develops with people you love and live with.

A person who claims to be a follower of Jesus claims to have a relationship with him. This means they know *him*, not just *about* him (this was Paul's claim in Philippians 3:10). Yet **we have turned our churches into groups of people who are studying God as though they were taking a course at school or attending a business seminar. We aim at the head. We don't deal in rela-**

tionship. And we wonder why there is no passion for Jesus and his mission? It's because, in our efforts to disciple people, we've been barking up the wrong tree.

Wrong Question: How Do We Develop Church Members?

The pursuit of this question makes good sense if the issue is getting people converted to the church, if living a Christian life is considered mainly to be about supporting church activities, if the assumption is that the primary expression of one's talents and gifts is at the church or in support of church programs, if the operating premise is that following Jesus is about joining a church and adopting a church member lifestyle, if we believe that people will grow more like Jesus by hanging out at church, if we want the measure of a person's spiritual maturity and "commitment" to be counted in institutional terms. These assumptions are frightfully prevalent in the church culture. And even more frightening, they may be preventing people from entering the kingdom.

Consider what most churches hand people when they join the church: a new-member packet. What's inside? Offering envelopes (the clear message: club dues are payable immediately and regularly), a church directory (sometimes with pictures of fellow club members), a church calendar (a list of club activities), a church officer and committee list (these are the important club members), and a constitution and bylaws (club rules). Also included in many packets are "opportunities for service"—usually a listing of church jobs that need doing.

The new-member packet signals to recipients what's really important—how to work your way into the club and get the most out of club membership. In the old days denominations and church consultants even offered courses on "member assimilation." People don't want to be assimilated. But that's what it feels like for many people who joined the church only to become part of "the collective" and lose their own individual lives.

We have made following Jesus all about being a good church member. The scorecard is all about church membership, church participation, and church support. We are training people to be good club members, all the while wondering why our influence in the world is waning. The truth is, the North American church culture extracts salt from the world and diminishes the amount of light available to those in darkness who need to find their way.

Jim (not his real name) asked if he could talk with me for a few minutes. He began, "I just feel like something is missing in my spiritual life."

"Tell me about your spiritual journey," I responded.

"I believe in God," he stated, and then for the next ten minutes detailed a fabulous club member dossier. This man had "joined the church" when he was young. He had held many positions of leadership: Sunday School teacher and director, deacon chairman, pastor search committee chairman; the list of committee appointments was impressive. This man obviously had worked hard in the church and had the respect of his fellow church members. Then he repeated, "But something is missing."

"Jim," I said, "in this whole discussion you mentioned God once, saying you believe in him. The devil can say that. You've not mentioned Jesus at all. Could it be that Jesus is what you're missing?"

Many churchgoers, like Jim, feel as though they've been sold a bill of goods. They have been told if they will only conform to church culture expectations, they will experience a wonderful Christian life. In fact, the sermons they hear talk about God some (or a lot) and even suggest that they are supposed to be experiencing abundant life. They have shown up, given, supported, studied—and they keep waiting for their ship to come in. They truth is, they feel cheated. They feel as though they've been promised something that they haven't gotten. And many of them are experiencing a growing crisis of belief—not just about the church but also about God. They know their life is not much different or no different from those of people who have Sundays free to spend with their families and give to charities they believe in. Although many church observers point to this as an indictment of church members, I see this as an indictment of the church culture.

I don't think the answer is to raise the bar for church members in terms of institutional support. **I think the solution is an abandonment of the church culture idolatry and a radical reintroduction of spiritual formation.**

Tough Question: How Do We Develop Followers of Jesus?

A friend of mine once asked me, "What is this kingdom business you keep talking about?"

"The kingdom is people," I replied. People are built to last. The Scriptures say that every other created thing is eventually gone. When the kingdom fully comes, people will finally realize their full potential as beings created in the image of God. Jesus hinted at this when he spoke about abundant life. To live abundantly is to borrow the future into the present. This means that helping people develop emotionally, physically, and relationally is all spiritual. There is no sacred-secular dichotomy when it comes to spiritual formation. It includes personal spiritual disciplines, but it also includes the stewardship of our relationships, our work, and our life mission.

This question changes everything. It challenges our beginning assumptions in the church business and it snaps tension and accountability into the evaluation of what we do in terms of the end result of helping people grow and develop. What if, when pastors get together, the question they asked each other was not, "How is your church doing?" (This is the most frequently used pickup line used at church leadership conferences and denominational gatherings.) In my denomination it's, "How's your Sunday School doing? or music program? or youth program?" or any number of other programs. The church culture has trained church leaders to have these conversations. Almost all the questions for denominational research and reporting are about church institutional life: how many showed up, how frequently, how busy they were in church activities, how much did they give, and so forth. This is how we keep score and determine champions, division leaders, and losers. What if, instead, we asked about people, not the institution? What if denominational reporting inquiries asked, "What percentage of your congregants feel they grew to be more like Jesus this past year?" What if church leaders asked each other, "How is God at work in your people?" or "Where do you see Jesus bustin' out?"

As part of a denominational futuring process a couple of years ago, we interviewed hundreds of South Carolina Baptists. We asked them about their "heart hopes" for the future. Although they wanted to see more people coming to church, they registered a very clear aspiration for themselves: they want to grow at church, not just put in time. The feedback was so significant that the futuring group fashioned an initiative that said we would help every congregation implement an intentional spiritual strategy for its constituents. My colleagues and I knew we would have a tough time communicating this initiative because church leaders think this is a given. All that's necessary for people to grow as a Christian, they think, is to offer the typical array of church educational programming. Unfortunately, people aren't growing like they want to or so many people wouldn't be begging to experience it.

Based on what we discovered in our heart hopes sessions, our convention (the South Carolina Baptist Convention) reorganized our staff in part to give attention to this need. We moved away from a program model staffing plan (consultants for Sunday School, Discipleship Training—the denominational educational programs) and created a Congregational Spiritual Development Team with consulting services offered around life stages: adults, youth, college, preschoolers, children. The only reservations to the change came from, you guessed it, church culture leaders who can only think in institutional, program terms. "What happened to Sunday School?" they asked. They see the Sunday School (a church program) as the point rather than the issue being the church's offering Bible study or the church engaging in intentional people development.

Lessons from the Y

A few years ago my family became charter members of a new YMCA that was being built near our home. I had never belonged to a health club before. One reason was that those exercise machines have always intimidated me. They look like implements of torture (and the looks on the faces of the people using them confirmed this). I was embarrassed that I knew so little about the equipment when everyone else there seemed so much at home.

This is exactly the same dynamic experienced by people outside the church bubble when they consider coming to church. They don't know the right code words, secret handshakes, or anything. They don't understand "church-speak." I am convinced we use code words and phrases in church to keep from dealing with God. Last night, after I pleaded passionately with a congregation about the need for renewal of the North American church, the pastor got up and said, "Thank you for the challenge. I hope we will all go out and apply this to our lives." I wanted to scream! What an innocuous response! So typically churchy. We pretend to be serious by offering some platitudinal phrase about "challenge" or "commitment." I would have rather the pastor had gotten up and said, "I think this man has overstated the case and I'm not nearly as discouraged as he is," or "I think this guy is full of Brussels sprouts," or "I can't believe anyone paid by our denomination would say such things," or something that meant something. Instead, church-speak allowed the listeners to avoid genuine accountability. The pastor gave the members permission to return to spiritual somnolence. I believe I heard the rhythm of snoring return as they shuffled out.

Back to the Y. I overcame my tentativeness about my lack of upbringing and joined when the Y opened up. As part of the deal, the Y gave me the opportunity to make an appointment with a personal trainer. I could tell him what I wanted to accomplish in that room with all that equipment in it. He could then customize a personal training schedule to help me realize my objectives. For the next few months I watched as fellow health enthusiasts carried small clipboards around with them as they moved from machine to machine. Each of them had been given their prescribed exercise regimen on cards. Some intriguing things happened. Some people shrunk parts of their bodies. Others bulked up. Still others moved some body mass around. One day while watching Jason (the trainer) take another new inductee through an orientation I thought, what if the church took this same approach?

Let's return to that person or family who has just become a follower of Jesus and has joined a congregation or is considering becoming a part of church life. **Instead of dumping a packet of church club member stuff on them, why not interview them about what they would like to see happen in their lives in terms of their spiritual development and personal growth?** Maybe they've never thought in those terms. (Club members who have practiced churchianity for years would have more difficulty with this interview than spiritual seekers. Can't you just imagine how many paragraphs of church-speak a person could generate to keep from saying anything that could lead to accountability?) Once a life coach or spiritual development coach completed this interview, they could then fashion a customized personal growth strategy for the person or family. This developmental strategy could pull from all the things the church offers currently. The coach might say, "Based on your interests, we recommend the Tuesday morning ladies' Bible study and suggest you check out the group that ministers once a month in the juvenile detention facility downtown," or whatever. This could be done for each family member. What if the coach then said, "Let's get back together in a month (and maybe every month for some period of time) to check on your progress"?

Imagine the difference in how this would come across to the new member. Instead of signaling to them that they are to find their way into church stuff and make the church successful, the focus is completely turned around. The church treats them as a market of one, convincing them that the church is there to help them develop an abundant life promised to them by Jesus.

Benefits of Life Coaching for Spiritual Growth

Just this morning I reached the voice mail of a friend. On her message she identified herself as a counselor and life coach. (She and I had talked about her adopting the life-coach role long before Dr. Phil came on the scene.) She will be joined by many more in the therapy world who want to move away from a clinical approach to counseling to more proactive intervention.

The traditional life-coaching medium was parenting. We all know that parenting has been on the decline over the past few decades. We used to talk in terms of "reparenting" people to help them readdress life issues that sabotage their development. We are now talking in terms of "parenting" people who have never been parented. Talk to any student minister. They are dealing with many kids who have raised themselves. I'm not just talking about street kids; I'm talking about kids living in suburban neighborhoods who have everything material but have been shaped more by MTV than by their parents. Talk to military officers who deal with eighteen- and nineteen-year-olds who are coming to them largely unformed.

I am recommending that churches provide life coaching for people. We need to view this as spiritual formation. We cannot take the approach that we just need to teach people the classic spiritual disciplines, assuming that a person already has a developed center. We must use spiritual disciplines to help people form the center. We must attend to their self-awareness and life relationships. The process starts with that interview just described in the previous section. And by the way, you wouldn't have to wait until a person decides to become a member. Life coaching could happen whenever the person signaled they were ready. It can start when they are children. It can target individuals or family units.

If your church pursued life coaching for people, you would accomplish at least seven things:

1. You would be communicating to the person that personal growth and spiritual development are anticipated and even expected.

2. You would convince them of your enormous care for them and that the church is there for them rather than expecting them to be there for the church.

3. You would be doing research to determine what needs and hopes the church should be addressing. If a bunch of people were asking for the same thing, it would signal a new development need or a new ministry opportunity. This would be a very different approach from beginning church ministry planning with calendars and budgets.

4. You would strengthen the intentionality of what you are doing in terms of congregational activity and programming. If, over time, you noticed that a particular activity was not effective in helping people grow, you could quit investing staff time, money, facility use, and so forth, in it and reallocate the resources into something that brought more return on investment.

5. You could use this as an opportunity to introduce people to and educate them about spiritual disciplines and dynamics of spiritual growth. Jason, the Y trainer, gives a tour of every machine in the fitness room to health club neophytes like me. The reason is simple. As a newcomer to that world I didn't even know some of the possibilities available to my body through these machines until I was made aware of them. The same is true for people in the spiritual world. Many people in church have never encountered the disciplines of prayer, fasting, Bible study, and ministering to others. We assume people will pick these up along the way if they just hang out in the church long enough. That's like thinking that if I'll just go down to the Y once a week, hang out with other club members, attend meetings, eat doughnuts, drink coffee, and watch others work out, I will look like I've been exercising. The reality is that if I want the benefits of exercise, I

will have to get on those machines and sweat, grunt, and contort my face (apparently that helps to gain the benefits of a workout regimen). **The Y staff would never say, "He's a faithful and committed member" and consider it a success if I showed up regularly but didn't exercise. Yet we do this all the time in the church culture.**

6. You could prescribe growth regimens for people that intentionally infuse spiritual development in activities they are already pursuing. The process of life coaching could further the development of a missionary force by helping people see that God has already placed them in a job, neighborhood, relationship, or life assignment where their gifts and influence can be developed as they partner with God's redemptive mission in the world. It is absurd that schoolteachers who have contact with dozens of students every day be underdeveloped as to their missionary potential. They usually have more face time with students than anyone else (even parents). Why in the world would we do anything that would make them feel or believe they have to pursue their personal spiritual development down at the church and away from the classroom? The same would be true for a shop owner who employs workers, or a manager who supervises other people's lives, and so on. It would even be true for families. Didn't Jesus slam the Pharisees for failing to take their religion home? He disparaged their practice of tithing to keep their institution alive while ignoring needs even in their own families. Imagine helping people see how God can get into the life they already have instead of asking them to give up their life for the church.

7. You could leverage growth into other arenas of life in addition to the spiritual domain. People often need help in life issues that, though they do not exclusively represent a spiritual need, carry spiritual implications. Financial planning needs to replace stewardship education in most congregations, for instance. The church should address a wide range of life concerns, including life skills (parenting, cooking, sewing), relationships (blended families, marriage and family issues), and health concerns (exercise, nutrition,

even pharmaceutical awareness). Living has become so frenetic for many people that life gets pushed to the side, postponed for some future time when we have time and energy to pursue it. One of the real benefits of life coaching could be in helping people "get a life" by helping them with their decision-making processes.

I suspect there are people in every congregation who could be helpful as life coaches. In most cases life coaching will occur in a variety of relationships and venues in the congregation. But it will not occur unless we free up people and time to do it. This means less church activity and more people development.

An Agenda for Spiritual Formation

The deal is this: **we have assumed that if people come to church often enough they will grow.** We've got to be much more intentional than this. The current approach to spiritual development focuses on the members' involvement in church activity. What if we took out a clean sheet of paper and asked, "What do we want people to learn?" and then went to work on this? We might even need to call off church to get some of these things done (as long as we collect the offering).

Worship

People are built to worship. Just go to any college football stadium in the fall of the year. You will see tens of thousands of avid worshippers. I do not disparage this. I am saying we need to learn from this. People will worship something! In football stadiums the bands and cheerleaders coach people into worshipping, not by giving directions but by worshipping themselves. Their worship coaxes others to join in. Every worship leader, instrumentalist, band member, and vocalist needs to understand that their primary responsibility in the stadium is to worship God. They need to understand the contagious nature of worship and the critical role it plays in missional renewal of the church. There is hardly anything more evangelistically powerful than a group of worshiping believers.

Apply Biblical Truth to Life and Relationships

Jesus promised abundant life. Why do we settle for less? We have separated people's heads from the rest of their bodies in church and aimed our spiritual "education" to hit them above the shoulders. We have believed that if people get enough Bible information it will automatically transform their lives. Wrong! **The devil knows more Bible than most church members in North America and can sign off on our doctrinal statements, but this knowledge has not transformed him.** Jesus told the Pharisees that they didn't get the point in their study of the Scriptures. "You diligently study the Scriptures because you think that by them you possess eternal life. These are the Scriptures that testify about me" (John 5:39, NIV). These Bible scholars missed the point. The point is Jesus!

Our approach to biblical study must not stop short of applying to life. Bible study for the head only leads to arrogance and dangerous religious bigotry. It misses the main truth. The Bible is the story of God's determination to woo human beings with his heart so he can transform them with his love and partner with them in his redemptive mission in the world.

Minister to Others in Jesus' Name

Both parts of this statement are crucial. Ministry to others keeps our experience with God from becoming merely a consumerist activity. It is the antidote to the self-absorption and self-centeredness that threatens to further privatize our American culture.

Equally key is the idea of ministering "in Jesus' name." This is the missional expression of the love of God. To give to others in Jesus' name is not an imperialist act but a loving introduction to the main truth about God's interest in people. His main goal is a loving relationship, not to control people's behavior. Love changes people's behavior. There are ways I serve my wife because of my love for her, not because she has a list posted on the refrigerator door of ways I need to behave. Unfortunately, many people see God this way. They see him as someone trying to gain entrance into their lives just so he can post some rules. What if we communicated to church members that Jesus elevated having love for our neighbors to the level of the second commandment, superceded only by the command to love God? What if every small group, every Sunday School class, every task group, and every believer were coached into ways to minister in Jesus' name, not as an add-on activity but as central to their spiritual development?

Share the Faith with Pre-Christians

Part of the spiritual formation of followers of Jesus surely should involve helping them know how to introduce Jesus into conversations and be able to pass along pertinent insights to people who are being drawn to God. Because we have made evangelism a sales activity in the North American church, we have reduced how much of it goes on. In many cases, we're not peddling Jesus— we're peddling the church, with the assumption that if people will come to the church and convert to churchianity they will get Jesus. What they often get is a poor substitute. **Evangelism that will introduce Jesus to this culture will flow from people who are deeply in love with Jesus.** It has happened before—in the Book of Acts. Their relationship with Jesus was what the early Christian community had to share with the world. They didn't have a Roman road, a New Testament, or any doctrinal treatises or "plan of salvation." They had Jesus. And people knew it. Their love for him turned the world upside down.

Cooperate and Partner with Other Believers in the Mission of God

Christianity was never intended to be a private affair. Community is something we find in the nature of God himself (the Trinity).

Belonging to others is part of a healthy expression of life. God's designs for humanity include family, and he is building a family to enjoy for eternity. Since Abraham God has been in search of a people who will partner with him in sharing his story with others. Part of spiritual formation is learning to be part of this family, including committing energy to other family members and sharing possessions, giving money to the cause, doing family chores (somebody has to do dishes at family feasts).

The communal aspect of spiritual formation is often neglected in a North American culture that has too often turned church membership to consumerism. The vast majority are there to get what they can, while a few with the need to serve or who have overactive responsibility glands pour on the work. This situation is a far cry from a healthy church life where each person would be contributing to others for his or her own growth. Our strengths, our gifts, and our talents are also our needs. If we have a talent to sing, draw, arrange, communicate, and so forth, we need to do this in order to grow and find fulfillment.

"School" in the Emerging World

In the modern world, how would we typically approach the spiritual learning objectives we've just identified? We'd write a curriculum, produce a conference, convene a class, create a study course, recruit a teacher or other expert, sign people up, teach the material to the students, and pass out completion certificates. Then we would wonder what would happen or change as a result of the experience. The truth is that we have very little evidence that academic or conferential learning changes behavior.

Just today a colleague with a new assignment punctuated how deeply steeped we are in this old approach to learning. My coworker has the responsibility for facilitating prayer for spiritual awakening throughout our state. He wants to mobilize people all over South Carolina to pray for the outpouring of God's Spirit. He and I have talked about some of the ways he will foster this movement. This past week he has begun to receive pressure to "have a conference" on prayer. This is the way typical denominational types think and act. (Let me ask you: If the world could be changed through conferences and seminars, wouldn't it have happened a long time ago?) We don't need a conference on prayer. We need people to pray! People don't need notebooks on how to pray for spiritual awakening; they need encouragement to seek the heart of God. Before it's over, if we follow the typical path, we'll wind up with "certified" prayer warriors. I'm sure this will help God sort out which petitioners to listen to.

I had lunch with a pastor yesterday who asked me to help him figure out a development plan for his senior ministerial staff. He didn't ask me to come to his church to share my expertise with his staff. He asked me where I would suggest he send his staff members in their various roles to experience top-flight ministries. My contribution was to help him get in touch with practitioners. My value was in helping to frame the learning agenda, then brokering learning opportunities. I was a learning facilitator. This is often the role of interventionists in the new reality.

These two examples serve to introduce some of the significant shifts we must take into account if we want to help people grow in the emerging world.

From Teaching to Learning

The academic model for the last several hundred years involved an expert (teacher) who had information and disseminated it to less-informed people (students). This was the basic plot that developed into millions of episodes of death-by-lecture.

This story line is increasingly disintegrating in its believability. Students can now obtain more information over the Internet overnight than a teacher can deliver in lecture form in a month's time. The issue now is *learning,* how to make sense out of the information that is available. **The agenda is more and more being set by the learner.** In the emerging world learners will decide what they want to learn, when they want to learn, and how they will learn (on-line, face-to-face, text, project, and so on).

From Curriculum and Text-Driven to Life-Driven

In the modern world spiritual formation was thought to be accomplished by taking a student through a prescribed group of texts that addressed topics in a curricular approach. This is so deeply ingrained in us that we approach almost any learning experience in the church this way. **Only in the modern world would you find people huddled together reading literature produced by mission agencies as a primary approach to mission "education" or would you convene a conference for people to spend all day taking notes in a notebook on fasting and prayer. This feels "normal" to us.** In the world that is dawning, the curriculum approach to growing people is increasingly viewed as a supplemental strategy to the primary approach: learning agendas driven by life issues and informed by life experiences.

Jesus facilitated spiritual formation in his disciples by introducing them to life situations and then helping them debrief their experiences. He taught them to pray. He did not lead them in a study course on prayer. He took them on mission trips (Samaria, for example); he didn't read books to them on the subject of missions. He sent them on learning junkets and exposed them to situations. He asked their opinion on what they were hearing and observing ("Who do you say that I am?"). He asked for radical obedience from them. He asked them to take up a cross and follow him. He did not send them to school and wait for them to graduate before giving them a significant assignment. He sent them out before they were ready to go and then helped them learn from their experiences. He talked about the kingdom of God, but mostly he lived the kingdom of God, practicing a life in front of his followers that modeled very different core values than those given to them by the Pharisees in the synagogues.

Helping people grow, particularly in the arena of spiritual formation, is about unpacking life: challenging our emotional responses that are destructive (envy, hatred, bitterness); challenging our biases (racial prejudice, social and economic elitism, intellectual snobbery); challenging our assumptions ("my needs are the most important"); challenging our responses; unpacking our frustrations, our hopes, our dreams, and our disappointments; bringing life to God rather than teaching about God, somehow hoping to get him into our life.

Curriculum-driven is artificial; life-driven is organic. Curriculum-driven is arbitrary; life-driven is circumstantially sensitive. Curriculum-driven is categorical; life-driven is personal. I am not suggesting that curriculum has no place. It does. In my experience with small groups, curriculum does help to convene the spirit of the learners to focus the discussion or prompt a place to begin. Curriculum in its best use provides a stage upon which learners can launch their own life stories for review and learning.

I believe in the power of community in learning, particularly in helping us make behavioral applications of what we learn. That is why I am such a proponent of small groups. The consistent challenge I run into when discussing small groups is the prevalent notion that small groups should function primarily in a curriculum mode (a Bible study, text-driven experience). This is why groups can move from one curriculum piece to another and never experience any real growth. Effective groups where people grow allow people to declare to each other what is going on in their lives, what they'd like to see going on in their lives, and what kind of help and accountability they need to move toward their hopes and away from their frustrations. This brings life to the table, not a book!

From Classroom to Living Room

In the new world the place of learning has shifted from the classroom (academic model) to the living room (life learning). On-line learning is just one expression of this shift, allowing people to engage learning from their homes at their convenience. It also shows up in the rising popularity of small group experiences that meet in homes, office buildings, bookstores, at the health club (wherever "living" is going on). It is why innovative companies are providing less institutional "canteen" space and conference rooms and more space like coffee bars and dens where staff can interact and share ideas. At the building where I have an office we are renovating space right now for staff that is off-limits to visitors; it is a "family room" where staff can hang out. I predict we will eventually renovate some of our sterile conference areas into more relaxed spaces, using lamp lighting rather than fluorescent fixtures, with coffee tables rather than conference tables.

This shift raises the question of why churches spend millions of dollars building file cabinets to put people in for an hour or two each week (we call it "educational space") when the most effective spiritual formation does not occur in these settings. The local church already has more Sunday School space than it needs, and people are already paying for it. It's called a home mortgage.

The issue in spiritual formation is bigger than just location. It involves a philosophy of where spiritual formation is centered. In the modern world spiritual instruction was owned and operated by the institution of the church. In premodern and postmodern cultures the home was and is the center for spiritual formation.

The student ministry where my family attends already knows about this shift of spiritual formation into living space. The students meet in homes throughout the week (mostly Sunday evenings) for small group discipleship. The small groups are convened by leaders whose primary requirement for the assignment is that they love young people and are willing to coach them in their life development (in other words, they are not recruited as teachers). The groups are noncurriculum driven. They focus on the lives of individual young people who talk about their spiritual journeys, challenge one another for growth, pray for each other, and receive encouragement. They provide the questions that prompt the God-answers. The setting in homes is critical for creating the kind of atmosphere and environment where these kids will open up and share their life struggles.

A second practice in this student ministry is also headed in the right direction. The student minister provides to parents each week a synopsis of the topics covered in the large group worship and teaching times, along with some questions the parents can use to help create conversations with their teenagers about spiritual issues. This moves them past the "How was church today?" question. I am amazed at how our best church families have no clue as to how to have conversations at home about spiritual subjects.

Churches are so busy getting people involved at the church that they've neglected this fundamental agenda of spiritual formation. The typical church family leaves spiritual stuff to what happens at the church, thereby delegating spiritual formation to the institution. And the institution encourages it! What if churches cut down on church activities so people could have some conversations within their own families? What if we facilitated this even at church as a beginning point? What if parents spent as much time with the children's minister as the children do? What if student ministers spent as much time with students' parents as they did the students? This would be a shift for most church expectations of staff. We typically hire children's and student ministers to run programs for children and young people. In fact, this approach by the church may do more to decimate the home as a spiritual center than anything coming into the home on television or the Internet.

From Didactic to Experiential

The effectiveness of most educational "experiences" has little to do with the student; it is mostly about the teacher's communication abilities as evidenced by students' test scores. We cannot afford this teacher-centrism in a church mission to help people grow. The issue has to be whether any life transformation is occurring; more specifically, disciples need to have a sense that they are growing spiritually by giving evidence of personal development. This means learners making personal investments, interacting with other learners, being open to coaching and accountability, and being able to "participate" in their own life learning.

Cathy, my wife, recently conducted a spiritual encounter session for pastors' wives at a retreat. She "sacralized" a hotel conference room by setting a couple hundred votive candles around the perimeter of the room. After a brief time of corporate worship the participants were allowed to customize their experience with God by being able to visit one or more stations that had been set up for them. One station included a collection of crosses and communion ware. Another station presented participants a pile of stones that could be moved from one spot to another to symbolize releasing a problem to God. Another station provided paper, art brushes, paints, and drawing pencils for those who wanted to write, paint, or draw. Still another section was available for special prayer intercession by a leader. The worship experience was actually customized by the participants themselves. Their experience reflected their need at that moment.

From Privatized Learning to Team Learning Environments

Maybe there was a day when it made sense for people to engage in privatized learning (in academic settings, even competing against each other for grades). But in a connected, relational economy the key to individual success is no longer an individual matter—it's about teams. So why shouldn't our educational methodology match up to the challenge that confronts us all— working with other people to accomplish life? Certainly in the arena of spiritual formation the developmental process preferably involves other people. Other people provide the challenge to character development. (I remember making the discovery after I got married of how impatient I was. It was much easier to be patient before someone else had a claim on the same time I did.

That wasn't the only character deficiency that surfaced, but I'm too modest to go into all that.)

Team learning environments involve small groups when people covenant together for growth. It also involves mentoring relationships, from the one-on-one to the one-to-three or whatever ratio. Team learning also occurs in ministry teams in which people work together on ministry tasks or projects. You can find out a lot about yourself when you work with people who have personalities or ideas very different from yours.

From Scripted to Shaped

In the modern world of mass standardization, education became scripted and curriculum based. Degree programs are still put together by curriculum requirements, often with prerequisites governing when you can take what. All students proceed at the same pace. You start in August, have exams in December, and after a prescribed number of courses you graduate. This is what I mean by scripted. In the emerging world the learning development process will be more shaped than scripted. This possibility is conceivable because of the information revolution, the ubiquitous availability of the information that used to be locked up in textbooks, classrooms, and teachers. Learners will proceed at their own pace (why should you have to wait for the whole class to get it?) and learn the way they learn best.

Sitting across from me just this minute is my college freshman daughter. I am writing and drinking coffee while she has tea and calculus. When she closed her calculus book I casually asked, "You finished?" She replied, "All I had to do was read." Then she added, "Why don't they write math books so someone like me (a more hands-on, practical, concrete learner) can understand them?" I followed up, "So how will you learn what's in there?" She sighed. "I'll have to get my roommate to explain it to me or work a few problems in class." For her, math needs to be a team sport (she won a savings bond in elementary school as part of a math team in a competition—it's the last time math was fun and easy for her to grasp).

The implication for spiritual development is pretty obvious. The spiritual formation process should be customized and shaped to the learner for intentional outcomes. We see this in the Bible. God dealt differently with Moses than with Peter, Paul, and Judas. The person development process is highly labor intensive. God works through all of our lives to shape us into the person he dreams we could be. **The community of faith should be an environment where the number one pursuit is the development of human beings created in the image of God and redeemed into his family through Jesus.**

Today I heard about a group of eleven ten-year-old boys who attend the same church I do. They have adopted a name for themselves—Band of Brothers. They have made a pact with each other to hold each other accountable all the way through junior high and high school. Included in the items of accountability are abstaining from alcohol and drug use, treating girls right, and incorporating some spiritual disciplines into their lives. They have given each other permission to coach and encourage each other in personal life development. They have created a learning community among themselves. The topic: life. They have captured the dynamics of creating an environment that helps people develop.

May their tribe increase!

New Reality Number Five

The Shift from Planning to Preparation

While on a trip to Hawaii I encountered the surfing culture. Surfers pretty well view everything else in life as paying rent just to get to surf. They get up before God rises and hit the water. They surf before they go to work and toss the board in the back of the truck or in the backseat (hanging out the window or sticking out through the sunroof) so they can be back in the water during lunch and after work. In the weeks I observed surfers I never saw one surfer plan a single wave, but I did see them prepare to ride the waves when they came.

God is making waves all around the North American church. Some churches are going to get to ride them. These are the churches that are prepared to get in on what God is up to. The North American church certainly did not plan the future we are talking about in this book, but church leaders can be prepared to deal with it.

Most of what has ultimate effect on the church happens outside of it and outside its control. No strategic planning group of any church in upstate South Carolina in 1990 made a note to check with Bavarian Motor Works to see where they were planning to locate their headquarters for North American production. But the decision by BMW to move into Greer, South Carolina, changed the whole area. The churches that prepared for the new world rode the wave of growth that came to the area.

Others continued to plan their way into cultural irrelevance, methodological obsolescence, and missional ineffectiveness in terms of being kingdom outposts.

Churches that will be left behind in the future are those busy answering the wrong questions. Among the wrong questions is one that deals with the way the church typically approaches the future.

Wrong Question: How Do We Plan for the Future?

Typical approaches to the future involve prediction and planning. This works OK in a world that experiences significant continuity. It doesn't work in the current environment for several reasons. If your predictions are off, your planning is off. Planning also tends to be incremental, pushing what we currently are doing into a world that we imagine will be the same as it is today. Incrementalism as an anticipatory strategy is dead. The growth of Internet technology, for instance, was exponential, not incremental, and it helped create a new world in communication that is vastly different from just a few years ago. A strategy of preparation makes much more sense in a world experiencing massive discontinuities.

The better (and biblical) approach to the future involves prayer and preparation, not prediction and planning. Spiritual preparation sounds like a passive activity to some people, involving sitting around in an "ohm" state hoping something will happen. This is a misconception. Let's return to the surfers for a moment. Their preparation to ride the waves involves a great deal of proactivity. They wax their boards, practice their stances, monitor the weather, get up early, and get wet. Hardly passive.

The Bible sounds a recurring theme: God wants his people to pray and to prepare for his intervention. It doesn't talk much about his people making plans and offering them up to him for his blessing (except in a negative sense—see James 4:14, 15). When God called Abram to begin a journey, he asked him to do something very nonincremental in the history of humanity's understanding of God. Because of Abram's obedience the world gained awareness of a monotheistic God who is interested in a personal relationship with human beings. This changed everything. No one could *plan* Abram's journey, including Abram (since he didn't know where he was going). But he could *prepare* for his trip. This involved informing the family of the move, wrapping up business, and pulling up tent pegs.

Consider the Exodus as another epic involving prayer and preparation. God called out to Moses from the bush that didn't burn up to say, "I have indeed seen the misery of my people in Egypt. I have heard them crying out. . . . So I have come down to rescue them" (Exodus 3:7, 8, NIV). (And God could have added: "By the way, I've been preparing you for this assignment for eighty years.") God planned Exodus. No human did. No one would have scripted the story the way God chose to do it. But even though they could not *plan* the Exodus, the Israelite slaves could *prepare* for it. Their job was to throw some blood around on the door to their houses, loot the Egyptians, order takeout, and watch for the e-mail signaling it was time to move out.

Look at the Incarnation from this same perspective. No one would have conceived a plan that involved a conception by a teenage girl of the Son of God. The visit of the second Person of the Trinity to planet earth in human form was hardly an incremental strategy! It was an interventionist strategy. The people couldn't plan it, but they could get ready: "*Prepare* the way of the Lord," thundered John the Baptist in the wilderness.

Consider Pentecost in light of our discussion. After giving the disciples the Great Commission, Jesus instructed them to go hang out together and pray. This was to prepare them for an intervention of God that they could not have imagined. The crew in the upper room was not engaged in a strategic planning retreat to plan the birth of the church and the early stages of the Christian movement. Not in their wildest dreams would they have scripted three thousand converts on Day One. Would they have predicted the leap of the Spirit to the Samaritans or to the Gentiles? Apparently not, based on their responses to both developments. Would they have recruited the rising star of Judaism to become the ultimate leader of the movement? Hardly. In fact, some evidence suggests that this group may never have had the vision to see the movement reach much beyond Jerusalem. But God had different ideas.

The anticipated Second Coming demonstrates the value of preparedness over planning. Jesus' consistent teaching in this area is for his disciples to be "ready," to be prepared. The parable of the wise and foolish virgins echoes this theme. The wise virgins get to go into the party because they are prepared. The others had a great plan: "Let's go to Sam's and buy a whole case of oil." They missed the party.

The difference between planning and preparedness is more than semantics in the biblical teaching. God does the planning; we do the preparing. It is God who declares: "I know the plans I have for you," he says in Jeremiah 29:11. He does not say, "I am waiting for you to develop plans I can bless." I am not against planning. I am just suggesting that there is a dimension beyond planning that is critical for us to understand. We can settle for our imaginations, our plans, and our dreams. In fact, I think the North American church has done just that. We have the best churches people can plan and build. But we are desperate for God to show up and to do something that only he can get credit for. God wants us to pray and to prepare for his intervention.

God knows, we need it.

Tough Question: How Do We Prepare for the Future?

Spiritual preparation has the goal of getting God's people in partnership with him in his redemptive mission in the world. It requires that his people say yes to him. "Let's consider it," "We need to vote on it," "We'll put together a study committee," are some of the things I hear church people say sometimes in order to practice incrementalism—to keep doing the same thing they've been doing (otherwise called disobedience). Saying yes usually comes about when God's people have had their hearts captured by his heart.

Spiritual preparation is not a formula. Nor is it a set of principles. It is not a program that comes in a kit. But it does have an architecture. In fact, these elements have a fractal quality about them, meaning that once these elements have been identified they are iterated and reiterated through every part of a spiritual effort or ministry organization. The five elements of a spiritual preparation architecture are vision, values, results, strengths, and learnings.

Vision

I remember when vision popped onto the scene in the conference circles of North American Christianity. I was teaching for the Fuller Institute of Evangelism and Church Growth at the time. Two things struck me in those early discussions: first, how visionless many church leaders were and, second, how the concept of vision was misunderstood. Two decades later two things strike me about vision and ministry. Guess what they are? We still don't get it, even though we talk about it a lot more. In fact, some people even think this is a tired concept. I have visited plenty of churches with the latest-great-idea-driven vision. They are full of tired and disillusioned people. **I suggest that people tire of visionless activity and organizations, but people never tire of vision,** that is, when it's the right one.

What Does Vision Do for You?

Genuine vision brings you some enormous benefits.

Vision Informs Your Decision Making. Though vision does not arrive from consensus, it inspires consensus. A guiding vision helps with both routine decisions and critical choices. Vision informs budgeting, staffing, ministry direction, building architecture, and strategies for outreach. Vision gives content to your church's message. It helps you establish brand recognition and supports the crafting of your corporate culture.

Vision can help reduce the number of decisions you have to make. I am amazed at the discussions that consume the time and energy of many congregations and church leaders. Some ideas should never garner a single ounce of energy. Some discussions should not even have to take place. Appropriate discrimination in and filtering of decisions is far more likely to occur if a leader and congregation have a resident vision.

One congregation has as their vision statement, "We are here to cause God joy." This theme permeates everything they do and how they do it. Their worship services are inspirational and celebrative; their stewardship campaigns are guiltless (but incredibly effective); their evangelism strategies are engaging. In all they do they are propelled toward a better future that happens when people get a vision of what it means to be people who cause God joy. Their decision making in every area of church life is informed by their vision.

Genuine Vision Engenders Commitment.   People are always committed to something. Vision captures commitment among people. It generates energy, fires up the imagination, and inspires excellence. I can tell you within minutes of arriving on a church campus whether or not a guiding vision is operative. Does the landscaping look like it's been left up to God to take care of? Does anyone greet me when I enter? Are staff members begging for volunteers? (I don't mean recruiting—that goes on in organizations with vision. I mean begging, badgering, cajoling, guilting people into service.) Are lackluster or mediocre efforts expended on ushering, singing, custodial services, teaching, signage, and so on?

This morning I drove to a church site in a part of the state unfamiliar to me. The church had no sign on the road or even on the church property. The only clue I had that I was at the right place was a church van in the parking lot with the church's name on it. Before I got out of my car I knew the congregation was not expecting any nonclub members to show up. Sure enough, what I discovered inside was a group of people content to grow older and fewer in number as long as they could enjoy their religious club meetings and keep member services paid for (including the chaplain "pastor" they hired to look after them). The pastor told me that new people to the area didn't feel welcome there. I never would have known!

In contrast, a pastor friend of mine pastors a congregation whose member and ministry efforts are fueled by a vision to be missionaries to their community. Everything from the artistry of the banners in the worship center to the fresh smell in the rest rooms screams that someone is paying attention. Every week scores of volunteers show up early to set up tables, put out literature, set up chairs, go through sound checks, and perform dozens of other tasks. These folks do it cheerfully, willingly, and enthusiastically. Their energy is palpable. Their commitment and excellence reflect the fact that they have been captured by a vision of community transformation, and they are eager to make their personal contribution to the effort.

Genuine Vision Creates Meaning. Today's knowledge workers need to know that what they do is significant. Companies that help their employees with this sense of significance create far more productive work environments. The same thing is true at church, because people act like people everywhere.

Genuine vision helps create a sense of significance in what people do. I was sitting on a bench on a beach boardwalk late one afternoon, resting after an hour walk. I had passed a woman in a green uniform pushing a broom several times. She came toward my bench doing her meticulous sweeping of the sidewalk. Suddenly she stopped, wiped her forehead, and rested on her broom. I called out to her: "You do a great job."

"Thank you," she replied. Then she added something that explained why the sidewalk behind her was spotless. "I just believe people want to walk on a clean sidewalk."

I was humbled to be in the presence of a worker who viewed her task with such significance. Whatever the park service was paying her, there's no way they could have demanded the excellence she brought to her work. That kind of motivation comes from within.

How Do You Cultivate Vision?

I find that many church leaders need real help in this area. Let me make some observations and suggestions.

Vision is discovered, not invented. In the old days of strategic planning we would lock a committee in a room and feed them bread and water until they crafted a vision statement. Starvation was the mother of invention. But God is the one with the vision for our lives and the church. It is our job to discover what he has in mind, not to invent something he can get excited about. People who don't consider themselves to be visionaries can take comfort in this.

How Do You Get Started in the Visioning Process?

There is no formula for this but I have several suggestions. First of all, *listen!* Listen to the heart hopes of the people you lead. Ask them what they would like to see God do in their lives and in the lives of the church and in the community. Listen to the leaders. Listen to the inner core. But also listen to the "fringe," the people who come infrequently (there could be a good reason for their nonparticipation). But don't stop with people in the congregation. Hold conversations with people in the community. Ask them what they would like to see happen in the community, what they perceive to be the greatest needs in the area, and how a church might help.

Second, to get started in the visioning process, *look!* Look at your town, your city. Look at where you are. Look at what's going on around you. (Who's moving in? Who's moving out? What businesses are starting or folding?) Look at the movies. Read the paper. Go to the bookstore and scan the titles of new releases. Ask what's selling. It's amazing what we don't see when we aren't looking! If you have to, rent another pair of eyes. Hire someone from the community who is unchurched to visit your church and ask her to debrief her experience. What did she see when she came?

Third, *talk* with your leaders. It's better to share your insights and your intuitions to see whether they strike a responsive chord with the people you lead. When you are speaking to them, pay attention to when you see the lights come on (does it happen when you employ a certain phrase, a sentence, an idea?) When do you sense the energy go up? What causes people to lean forward in their seats a bit? These responses are clues that you are on to something.

When she was a little girl, my younger daughter favored praying with her eyes open. One day I asked her why she did this. "So I won't miss anything!" she replied. This is the picture of what I mean about the vision discovery process. Pray with at least one eye open. Keep focused on God intensely while being firmly in touch with what's going on in the world you are assigned to minister to.

Who Should Develop the Vision?

I am moving more and more to a position that the pastor does not necessarily even need to be the chief architect of the vision. I have come to this position because so few pastors seem to possess this talent. If the pastor possesses this ability, then certainly it should be employed. But perhaps the pastor's strengths lie in communication or in pastoral care, not in visioning. Why not use the talents of others in this area? For this approach to work, a few things are essential. The pastor must be willing to submit to the manifest vision of God as revealed to the leadership team. The pastor must agree with it down into his bones to the extent that he is willing to shift behavior and priorities to pursue the vision. The pastor must be able to communicate the vision with clarity and passion, even if he is not the key architect. The way I say it is, the pastor must be able to compellingly deliver a compelling vision. This is absolutely critical. If the pastor has only one strong sermon, this has to be it.

I believe that taking the pressure of developing a vision off of pastors who are not good at it would promote higher-quality vision development. Right now, in many congregations, people are waiting for the pastor to come forth with a vision. Feeling this pressure the pastor reaches for the next great idea or borrows someone else's vision for the congregation. Why not put together a visioning team? Be sure to choose people who are future-friendly, Spirit-filled, and passionate about kingdom growth.

How Long Is a Vision Viable?

I frequently get this question or its close cousin, "How often should we revisit the vision?" Whereas a church's founding vision can have up to a generation of life, succeeding vision chapters usually last between seven and nine years. Since leaders are generally up to two years ahead of their congregation in terms of vision, they frequently begin to feel a restlessness between five and seven years into vision chapters. Some mistake this as their work being finished rather than understanding that this is a natural process of preparing them to begin the revisioning process.

In the emerging world people will increasingly demand intentionality in the organizations they belong to. They will only belong to those organizations that help them experience the vision they have for their own life. This makes vision all the more critical to the church for being able to recruit people into the great mission of God. To move beyond a program-based, activity-based approach to church life, church leaders increasingly will need to be able to cast a compelling vision of kingdom growth.

Values

Kingdom vision requires kingdom values to support it. Vision is the seed; values are the soil. I run into situations frequently in which the soil won't support the growth of the vision. Leaders who don't pay attention to clarifying values are often frustrated because they don't know why the vision goes nowhere. Make no mistake about it: competing value sets do not coexist peacefully. One set will win over the other. The clash between club member values and missionary values has claimed a lot of casualties.

Discovering Values

How do you know what someone's core values are? It involves more than what people *say* their values are. It's what people *do* that counts. **Values are demonstrated by behavior.** As the proverb goes, "What you do is what you believe; everything else is just religious talk." Occasionally someone tells me they don't know what their core values are. I tell them, "Go home and ask the people who live with you what they are."

In helping congregations identify their core values I run into a good deal of denial. Leaders will tell me what the congregation's values *ought* to be. I find out sometimes that the real values are something quite different. No church remotely acquainted with the tenets of the faith will tell you out and out that they don't believe in sharing the gospel, but many churches really don't believe in evangelism. If they did there would be fruit of it and behavior that supports it.

I suggest to congregations that they can discover their values from three sources. Start by asking people in the community to identify what the church stands for. Many congregations are surprised at what they discover. They either find out the church is known for something different from what they think or they find out the community is clueless about what the church stands for. This finding in itself is very revealing. It tells you that the church either is withdrawn from the community or not paying attention to its branding in the community.

A second source of core values is new members, after they've been a part of the church for six to nine months. They can tell you what they have experienced after the courtship period.

I also recommend to church leaders that they rent some non-church people unfamiliar with the church to visit for two to four weeks, then debrief their experience. What impressions did they form? Did people speak to them? Did the service make sense? Did they feel that they stuck out in the crowd? Was signage adequate? Did they encounter God? Were they inspired, challenged, and uplifted? What do they think the church is most interested in? Would they recommend the church to their friends? Would they come back if they were not paid to? (I know a lot of church staff who would answer "no" to that one!)

Practicing Values

Frequently I am asked whether a congregation can change values. Most business literature declares that corporate values cannot change unless you change the personnel. Typically this is hard for a congregation. It's hard to fire all the church members. I have known some situations where growth was rapid enough to shift the corporate culture, but that's relatively rare. So are we stuck with the values we discover, even if we discover that our values are nonbiblical and nonmissional? I don't want to give up without a fight. We are, after all, in the life transformation business, so I want to hold out hope that values can be challenged and can shift. But they won't change unless you know what they are to begin with and begin to practice new ones.

How do you practice values? The idea here is to strengthen values that support kingdom growth. I have four suggestions. First, you must create venues where people can practice the core values you espouse. Telling people they need to win the world for Christ, for instance, without giving them training, debriefing, and encouragement just engenders guilt among the troops, not more converts. **Practicing kingdom values may mean adjusting the church calendar to give people more time to participate in community or workplace ministries.**

A second way to practice values is through public deliberation processes that identify core values. This suggestion requires intentionality and discipline, and maybe even outside intervention in the form of a consultant or some kind of values-assessment instrument. (We use one with congregations who are beginning an intentional futuring process. It requires, at least, a public discussion of the core values and how they shape the congregation's ministry.)

The value of public deliberation of values came home to me early on during my days as the pastor of a new congregation. During one congregational meeting a member shared a concern about a family member who was soon to move to town. The woman told about a moral choice her family member had made that might make her unwelcome at church. I listened as several church members offered words of encouragement. They said they would welcome the person and love them without insisting that they first clean up their act. A young attorney eventually stood up to speak. He had joined the church with his family only the week before. "I just have one thing to say," he began. "If this is the kind of church I have joined," then paused for effect, "I have joined the right church." That pause seemed to go on forever, but it was worth the wait. People needed to have and hear that discussion among themselves. It helped set values that guide that congregation to this day, some twenty years later.

A third way to practice values is to engage in deliberate clarification of values in decision making. What if every recommendation from a ministry team had to be accompanied by a list of the values it champions? I think it would force a little accountability that could challenge the status quo. I was speaking at a church recently that was finishing the construction of a brand-new recreation facility. I said, "If you are like most churches, you have a committee meeting right now trying to figure out how to keep people from the community out of your building when it opens up." The light chuckle indicated what was confirmed to me later by the pastor. What if the facilities committee had to present their policies and procedures for booking the new facility accompanied by the admission that their recommendations promote club member values of closed fellowship, customer service for club members only, and refuge, just to name a few? That might just precipitate some conversation about what the values of a New Testament church on mission with God might include.

A fourth suggestion is that leaders must go first. It will mean the staff taking the lead, doing whatever it is they want to see happen. I remember listening to one staff group complain about the lack of community involvement on the part of their church members. I asked them about their own work habits and time allocations. As it turned out, they were all desk jockeys. Their behavior signaled to church members that ministry was primarily an office function done at the church. They could forget about motivating church members to be missionaries until they themselves changed behavior. Key lay leaders must also point the way.

When vision and values are in alignment, you have a powerful start toward being prepared to meet the future. Now the scorecard needs to be redesigned.

Results

Great leaders want results. Great organizations get results because they go for results and are willing to live and die by the results they identify as their benchmarks for success. Effective missional congregations are no exception. They know what constitutes success for them in God's eyes and they go after it.

Effective congregations keep score and they play to win. I am saying two things. First, you'd better have a scorecard to know when you are winning or the game is going to get pretty boring. Just take the hoops off the backboard and see how much fun it is to run up and down the court just throwing the ball up against the backboard. Or tell Olympic athletes that you aren't going to put the clock on them. After all, they're all winners. Are you kidding? The drive to achieve, make progress, and know when you are winning is a fundamental motivator for human beings, especially for champions.

A second reason that results are important involves the dynamic of playing to win. This approach is critical to success. You know the difference when individuals or teams play not to lose, instead of playing to win. They are overly cautious. They are not aggressive. They fail to perform to their best ability because their standard is just to be good enough to win against the next challenger. In contrast, those who play to win go all out, no holds barred, ears laid back, whatever analogy you choose. Even if they lose out to some other competitor, they are the ones who define the game, who make it a contest worth winning.

My spirit sighs at how few congregations play to win. They play just to have a few more than last Sunday or a few more than last year on this Sunday. They play to hang on to what they've got. They play to meet budget. They play to meet expenses. They play to do better than the church down the street, up the road, or across town (whoever they have determined to be their competitor). They play to fill up buildings and pay off the debt. They play to keep the doors open. They play to survive.

I am convinced that the reason for much burnout, lack of commitment, and low performance in our churches among staff and members is directly related to the failure to declare the clear results we are after. We don't know when we are winning. The North American church as a whole suits up to go out and take a drubbing, then retires to the locker room to bandage each other up and tell each other that the loss could have been worse. This has gone on so long that the team thinks this is normal. They prefer to keep playing the same old game with the same low expectations.

To make things worse, the coaching staff (clergy) has bought into this depressing plot. Their pep talks tell the team this is what they should expect. Their game book has no surprises in it. Their coaching philosophy (doctrine and theology) absolves them from responsibility for developing new plays or putting together a winning team. They blame their predicament on the team owner (God), poor fans (the culture), or on a lack of talent and commitment in the players (church members). They do not take responsibility for results because they do not have the emotional strength to risk pushback from the team if they put tension on them to win. Some of these coaches are so emotionally needy they have come to look at losses as relative wins. They go to coaches' clinics to cry on each other's shoulders, to "encourage" one another. If the truth were known, it makes them feel better to find someone else worse off than they are or, at least, to be reassured from other coaches that they are miserable also. Usually absent from these meetings are the winning coaches. This does not rescue them from the ridicule of those assembled, however.

The Relationship Among Vision, Values, and Results

Let me tell you how bad it has gotten. Whenever I begin to mention posting some clear results for people to work for, an interesting thing happens with many spiritual leaders. It is the same dynamic as throwing on a light in a room full of cockroaches. They run for cover. Many North American church leaders resist accountability at almost every level—personally and with their ministry efforts.

I can hear some of you saying now: "I knew it would all boil down to this—nickels and noses." Just hold on! I am saying that keeping score is critical. I have not said what the scorecard is to look like. You have been trained by the church culture to leap to the conclusion that buildings, budgets, and baptisms are the only bottom lines that count. I have not said that, nor will I.

What I will say is this: **the results you are looking for need to be informed by your vision and values.** This may involve (and probably will) some numbers, but they will be vital signs connected to what you have determined to be. For instance, I was consulting a church once whose vision statement said something about working to transform lives. I asked them, "How many of those animals do you have around here?" They began to backpedal. "Well, you know, God changes people over time; he looks in the heart, so only he knows how to gauge this."

"Hey!" I told them, "you are the ones who told me you are in the life transformation business. I just wanted to know if you had any results you could point to." I bring this up not to criticize their vision but to suggest that the hard work of translating it into results had not been tackled.

In contrast, another church that also declared they were in the life-changing business decided to design a scorecard that would be biased toward these results. They determined that although spiritual growth involves personal choices, they could take responsibility for creating the kind of environment that encouraged people to make these choices. So they decided on several initiatives, including creating a cadre of life coaches and providing personal growth opportunities. They established expectations for how the staff would contribute energy to this as well as how many people they would touch. They determined to help people assess their own personal development and established a results expectation that participants in their church ministry would register positive personal growth gains over time. The congregation's vision and values had an impact on the results they were serious about. The leadership took responsibility for what they could take responsibility for, and they went all out after it.

Celebrating Results

A fundamental truth about people systems will help you in establishing the results you are after: **what gets rewarded gets done.** This dynamic certainly holds true in churches.

Too many churches reward negative behavior, some even as a practice. One church made it a practice to give out critical committee assignments (personnel and stewardship, for example) to the members who had raised the biggest stink in the business meetings all year long. When I asked why, I was told that the members of the committee on committees felt this behavior demonstrated high interest in the church. This strategy, to me, is like going out into the body searching for cancer so you can pull it to the heart.

Some pastors allow people to act out in all kinds of ways, and actually pour on the attention when they create difficulties. Some unhealthy members have figured out that this is the easiest way to get attention. In many church systems there are no downsides to them for their behavior because they are not held accountable for their destructive ways. The corporate culture in these cases has become complicitous in feeding the piranha that rip and tear at the body of Christ.

The key is to reward the right behaviors so that you get the results you are looking for. It is critical that heroes be made of the right people and the right ministries that embody the vision and values of the congregation. One church began to get outside the church and into the neighborhoods in their metropolitan area. They were having some tremendous success in several initiatives. The trouble was, no one in the church was there to see these ministry breakthroughs. They devised a strategy to get some video clips of these successes and show them during the morning worship service. The senior pastor initially resisted, thinking this was "promotion." Eventually he understood the power of celebrating ministry successes to create more ministry successes.

Churches must search for ways to honor their missionary members by telling the stories of their kingdom contributions— on bulletin boards, on their Web site, in small group settings (Sunday School classes, growth groups, and so on) as well as in corporate worship settings. In most churches people who fix food for special occasions get more applause than people who introduce people to Jesus. (What club member values do you think this shows?) Why not include people in the baptismal ceremony who help bring people to Jesus or when they are introduced to the church?

Celebrating people is only one way churches reward what they want to see done. Others create special events to punctuate the results they are achieving. My home church makes a big deal out of baptism. They create a party atmosphere by serving hot dogs and popcorn and having fun. Sometimes they hold the service in a lake or a clubhouse pool as a public witness. They take a picture of the person being baptized, frame it for them, and present it to them. The truth is, we typically make more of a high school graduation in church than we do of people becoming part of the family of God. Don't get me wrong. We should applaud food service servants and recognize milestone achievements (like high school graduation). I'm just saying that we should also have a strategy to benchmark progress in achieving intentional results.

Designing the ministry scorecard is going to become increasingly important as congregations move to embrace the future described in this book. Actually, the process will be more of a redesigning. We have developed church scorecards that measure bottom lines only—attendance, giving, and membership. (It's a lot easier to design scorecards for bottom lines of attendance and money. I suspect that's why we have defaulted to this accounting.) We must move toward identifying the key processes and activities that will produce what we hope to see happen and begin to establish accountabilities around those. Merely reporting on the number of baptisms does nothing to increase them. We need to train people to share their faith, track the number of conversations church members are having with pre-Christians, and discover the number of pre-Christians who are being touched by the congregation's ministry efforts. Ideally, the scorecard will tell people what must happen to achieve the results you want.

To be spiritually prepared a church must be willing to turn the hoped-for future into intentional initiatives, activities, and processes. In other words, if the church will make clear the results they are looking for, they are positioned to experience missional effectiveness. They will be able to make tough decisions on the use of resources. They will be more likely to prioritize their efforts. They will be more intentional. They will be ready to catch the wave.

Strengths

As a component of a spiritual preparation architecture, strengths include both strengths awareness and strengths building. The focus on strengths as a preparation for the future runs counter-intuitive to what most Americans think. Most of us believe the best way for us to improve is to engage in some form of self-remediation (lose weight, stop a bad habit).

Our culture focuses on weaknesses. If a child comes home from school with a report card of four A's and one C, what does the discussion typically center on? Often we tell children they need to spend more time on the things that come the hardest to them, leaving underdeveloped those talents that are most natural. We do this because we have been taught that only what comes hard counts. So we wind up helping people spend lots of time trying to develop talents they don't have. We also try to "balance" people out. Balance is a myth. I do not know a single balanced leader. In fact, leaders by definition are imbalanced people. They are "out of round" in the areas of their passion, their giftedness, and their vision.

Your best shot at making your best contribution is for you to get better at what you are already good at. God called you, not in spite of who you are (this is such a prevalent view) but precisely because of who you are. Your strengths (the development of your talent with experience) provide a clue to your calling and ministry assignment. When we ignore them we degrade the work of God in us. When we focus only on fixing weaknesses we tell God his gifts are not an important part of who we are. Our efforts at mending ourselves are a form of idolatry, another evidence of our trying to be God. Only he has all the talent. I am talking about talent, not character, which we should obviously strive to improve.

In American business we tend to hire people for their strengths and then beat them up for what they're not good at. Consider the parable of Frank, the ace car salesman. He can sell cars like crazy; in fact, he could sell anything. But he's not too good with paperwork. So the Human Resources Department decides to fix him by focusing on Frank's weakness to round him out. They send him off to a paperwork seminar for a week. Just before he leaves for his trip they tell him they want him to teach what he learns to the rest of the staff when he returns (they want to make sure Frank goes to class and takes good notes).

In addition to having a lot of self-motivation (great salespeople always do), Frank also enjoys the habit of providing food for his family. So he pays attention, takes good notes, and comes back ready to reform his ways. This is the game face he brings back home from his experience. In case you're wondering what really happened, this week for Frank was a trip to Hades. His self-esteem took a beating for five days as his nose was rubbed in his weakness. He has had to face his lack of talent for hours on end and forego any celebration of his true contribution to the team. (If an NFL team sent their quarterback off to a kicking clinic, we would think they were crazy—and we'd be right!)

Back home, Frank does a great job "selling" his colleagues better paperwork techniques and habits (after all, Frank will apply his talent in any scenario). Management is convinced that they are geniuses and this is why they earn the big bucks.

That's when the problem begins. You guessed it. Frank's sales begin to slip. He is working longer hours because it takes him so long to do the paperwork. He is tired because the paperwork brings him no energy; in fact, just the opposite. Frank begins evidencing signs of burnout. Management calls him in. "Frank, what's wrong with you?" (Notice where blame is placed.) Frank's enjoyment of his work drops off right along with his productivity. When he loses his job he becomes another casualty to an ungodly approach to "developing" people—focus on their weaknesses. (Should you be wondering about reevaluating the message of the church at this point? **Do you think people are fundamentally problems for God to fix or child-creations to celebrate?**)

We create Frank's story at church all the time. We call staff members for what they bring to the table, then give them poor evaluations for what they told us to begin with that they weren't good at and didn't enjoy doing. We recruit volunteers for their strengths and then focus on what they don't get done to our satisfaction. **We create losers.**

Do not hear what I am not saying. I am not saying that we should ignore weaknesses. We should manage them. This means we figure out ways to minimize the impact of individual weaknesses on the organization so that a person's strengths are not compromised or nullified. Strategies might include recruiting to the weakness (hire Frank an assistant to do paperwork), outsourcing, or changing job expectations, to name a few. We obviously must address the most glaring weaknesses, those that threaten to derail our success. But there are fewer of these than you think. **The perfectionism of the North American church rears its ugly head here. It not only militates against grace, it also makes it hard for pastors, staff, volunteer servants, and leaders even to admit to weaknesses, thereby making it harder to celebrate their unique strengths and contributions.**

Developing a strengths philosophy in our churches would accomplish several things. First, it would call out and release energy for facing the challenges of the future. I am convinced that one of the reasons churches and church leaders have so little energy for prosecuting a missional agenda is our tendency to focus on weaknesses. A lot of burnout that churches and leaders suffer result from being engaged in prolonged trivia, doing things that don't matter and bring them no energy. Too many church leaders are paying too high a rent to get to do what they enjoy the most, what they are called to and gifted to do.

Most planning processes immediately go to work on a congregation's weaknesses. This is why, when you announce you are going to begin some kind of planning exercise, it conjures up the same enthusiasm that you would generate if you asked people to line up for a root canal. The process typically reminds everyone what the church is not doing well—and we wonder why it doesn't inspire people to action. One widely used church diagnostic piece asserts that a church will never rise above its greatest weakness. That's nonsense! People and organizations rise above their weaknesses all the time—if they build on their strengths.

An ice-cream place I go to has too little seating, too little parking, too high prices—but it's always packed! Why? Not because they are trying to fix the weaknesses I've just mentioned. Their business is phenomenal because their ice cream is beyond fabulous and they turn eating ice cream into a fantastic and memorable experience. (I still carry around my waist the memory of the visit.) My hunch is that their staff meetings focus on customer service, specifically how to help people enter into the thrill of creating a customized personal treat. This is the stuff they do best.

I know plenty of churches that have capitalized on their strengths in the face of glaring weaknesses. In fact, their strength is what fills in their brand content, gives them their ministry identity, and distinguishes them from the pack. One church I know is known for great worship. In spite of their lack of small group strategy, they continue to introduce people to Jesus. Another church is known for its work with overcomers, people who are struggling with drug and alcohol addictions and problems. They don't have the greatest teaching ministry, but their loving ministry is almost without peer. Both of these churches are constantly getting better at what they are good at. They are building on their strengths and making a great contribution to their communities.

Should these churches ignore their weaknesses? Of course not. They would certainly want to address these issues to the point that they do not hinder the church mission. They would be open to God's provision for these areas and be smart about strategies to improve. But if they followed many prescriptions for improvement, they would exhaust their energies in ways that would bring less return on investment than a strategy that figured out how to exploit their strengths even more. They would be well served to employ their strengths even in addressing their weaknesses. The church weak in small groups but great with worship would use the worship experiences to move people into contact with small group ministries. The second church would add teaching components to their recovery group life.

In a kingdom theology, could it be that one church actually serves a community better in worship, while one really contributes in Bible teaching, and so on? This is happening already, but we don't admit it in our individual congregation's scramble for market share. The North American church notion of "membership" assumes that churches hold exclusive claim on people's time, energy, money, and service. But this idea is collapsing in the face of what's going on. Increasingly we are finding people who "belong" to two or more churches. A young man on a plane recently recounted to me his involvement with four churches that he considered himself a part of (one for worship, one for mission trips, another for their teaching ministry, and a fourth for their need of his technical expertise). The reason church leaders don't understand this growing trend is the institutional implications: we don't know how to count this participation or take up the offering in this new kind of world.

A second benefit of adopting a strengths philosophy is that we would be cooperating with God in his designs for the church. What an idea! The gifts, talents, passions of the people of a congregation hold great clues to the plans and purposes God has for the group. I am convinced many churches forego their best contribution to people's lives and to the community by trying to be everything (or by trying to be someone else's idea of church for them) rather than being who God made them to be. This is a tough pill for people to swallow, but it betrays the idolatry in our own hearts and minds of "building" churches or "growing" churches—neither of which we can do ultimately. What we can do is be faithful servants to create and foster an environment where people can grow in their personal lives and where the people of God corporately and collectively can say yes to the mission God has for them in the world.

Designing a strategy for preparing for the future based on the congregation's strengths also upholds for people the value of celebrating their own strengths. This signals to maturing followers of Jesus that they should pursue a course of discovering their own talent and applying it to their life experience in order to live more intentional and abundant lives. The freedom in this approach would liberate enormous creativity and energy for pursuit of the church's ministry and mission.

If we would agree with God in his gifts to us, we would be much happier campers. People with joy make great recruiting agents for kingdom growth.

Learnings

Just because we don't know how to do something doesn't mean we shouldn't try to do it. Much of the incrementalism that plagues the North American church results from a failure to learn. Without the will to learn the church defaults to methodologies and mental maps that keep it anchored to the old world and tethered to outmoded paradigms. This anchor and rope is going to drag most churches into the abyss, cursing the waves rather than riding them.

The fact that we don't know how to turn members into missionaries, or how to redesign our ministry scorecard, or how to train leaders for the movement, and a whole bunch of other things I've talked about, shouldn't keep us from trying to figure it out. The truth is, we don't know how we are going to be church in the emerging world. We're going to have to learn. And we'd better get started.

In a spiritual preparation architecture, learning constitutes the fifth element. In the old strategic planning world, plans would call for periodic evaluation during the implementation phase. These evaluations would be periodically conducted after some stated time had elapsed. Assessments would be made to determine what was working and what was not. Adjustments would then be made in the plan, again to be evaluated for effectiveness at some later period. This approach will no longer do in a world of increasing fluidity. Feedback must be continuous in order for leaders of congregations to have adequate information for decision making and for determining the impact of these decisions in terms of missional effectiveness.

Church leaders must go to "school" all the time. Their course of study will depend on the challenges they face. I have already identified some key areas. A beginning list includes postmodernism, generational cultures, visioning, communication, organizational behavior and development, leadership development, team building, apologetics, and futuring, just to get started.

Your strategies for securing learnings are going to be as varied as the nature of the learnings you need to acquire. You will want to consider some pointers in charting your course.

1. *Go where it's happening.* Cultural studies may require going to the movies, hanging out at the bookstore, and renting a teenager or two (from outside the church bubble) to educate you to the youth culture (a look not at what's ahead but what's already here). You might need a NASCAR pit crew to teach you about team building.

2. *Get outside the box.* I am suggesting that you escape the typical learning orbits of most church leaders who limit their investigation only to what other churches are doing or what they have done in the past. One church staff leader who was fairly new to his church brought me his plans for his "new direction" to get my input. The material had his previous church logo on them! This guy was planning to do the same old stuff in a new location. Never mind that his old approach was alien to the culture of the new place. I am not against being up to speed in the

church industry in terms of knowing what's going on out there, but I am biased against pursuing a learning path that never leaves the church halls. The North American church is so self-absorbed that most inquiries will tend to perpetuate innovations in *doing* church, not *being* church.

3. *Don't pursue privatized learning.* You need to create a learning community for yourself (or multiple learning communities). Recruit three or four other leaders who share similar leadership challenges and worldviews to join you in your learning quest. Decide what you will learn together. Engage in your learning activities as a group and debrief your life and ministry with each other.

4. *Develop a chief learning officer.* Your congregation needs at least one of these. Actually you may end up having several. You may have one for technology, another for spiritual growth processes, and so on. The point is: somebody needs to be paying attention to learning opportunities and resources that would further the church mission. These learning strategies may target the leadership core, the church at large, or specific staff members, whatever is appropriate. You need to elevate these people to staff level if they are inside the congregation (either paid or volunteer) or hire them as consultants for your leadership if they are from outside the church. I would try to have this role filled by someone in the church if at all possible—probably a layperson or laypersons.

5. *Secure a learning coach for yourself.* You need a chief learning officer for your own company (that's You, Inc.). One of the key developments in executive management in recent years has been the emergence of the executive coach. If you are a spiritual leader, you need to cultivate one or more relationships that will serve you in this capacity. These people need to understand your life mission but also your learning style and your leadership challenges. They may or may not be people in the church world. They may be business consultants, community leaders, academics, even government officials. Get them wherever you can find them. When you find them, cultivate them. You may need to rent them, but this could be some of the best continuing education money

you can spend. Meet with them at least twice a year in person if possible or schedule a phone conversation if face-to-face is not practical. More will fall out of the conversations than you can use at any one time (or between coaching sessions), but you will be developing a portfolio of resources and learning opportunities for your lifelong development as a leader.

The future belongs to those who prepare for it, not those who plan for it. If the North American church is going to make the leap off the sigmoid curve and avoid the sure death guaranteed by incrementalism, it will have to shift its beginning point from the present to the future. This should not be so hard for spiritual leaders to understand. After all, Jesus taught us to pray, "thy kingdom come." That phrase is the fast-forward button in the Christian's prayer life. The kingdom is a future that is already present. Our mission is to introduce the kingdom into this world, with its preferred future for humanity.

The future is the best place to start.

New Reality Number Six

The Rise of Apostolic Leadership

God must have had a lot of confidence in you to put you on the planet at just this time. It was his sovereign decision to insert you onto planet earth during a time of huge transition. It takes incredible faith to lead during hinge points of history.

Think about John the Baptist as a transitional leader. He grew up hearing the stories of Luke 1 and 2 as part of his family legend. Can't you just hear John's mom? "When your daddy found out we were expecting you, he couldn't say a word!" or "When your Aunt Mary came to see me to tell me she was going to have a baby, I thought you were going to jump plumb out of me!" John saw heaven open and the Spirit descend when he baptized his first cousin. Yet when he was thrown in jail he sent word to Jesus, "Now, let's go over this one more time: are you the one?" Jesus doesn't slam John. In fact, he extols his cousin. "There's never been a better man born," Jesus says (Luke 7:28—again).

Jesus doesn't slam you either for your doubts, your fears, your uncertainties. He wants to encourage you in your current assignment. You are being asked to lead during a time when you are not sure where all this is going. If previous history is an accurate indicator, the kinds of changes we are undergoing will not settle out for another century or more. This means that some of you are giving direction to the great-great-great grandparents of the leaders of the Christian movement when it all shakes out on the other side of the postmodern wormhole. You are leading by faith, trusting that the subplot obediences you practice will contribute to the larger drama. Your courage to believe with partial sight will be rewarded one day when a full view is afforded.

On the flip side, you have the chance to do what only a few have been privileged to do. **You get the chance to give shape to the movement that will define its expression for perhaps hundreds of years (if Jesus doesn't come back and usher in the kingdom).** You must choose carefully.

Leadership is always in high demand and short supply. Sometimes the leadership deficit is more acute. This is especially true in times of great paradigmatic shifts, when the leadership requirements are shifting as well. It takes time for a new crop of leaders to come up to speed to the new set of challenges. We are in such a leadership crisis right now in the North American church. Simply put, we have a critical shortage of the right kind of leadership necessary to help the North American church become more missionally effective.

This new reality explores the kind of leadership God is raising up for the missional revitalization of the North American church. I will examine both the content of this leadership and the leadership development processes required to support it (both lay and clergy components). We are going to have to shift the leadership quest if we are going to experience kingdom growth.

Wrong Question: How Do We Develop Leaders for Church Work?

If church work is not getting the job done, why do we continue to train leaders to do it better? This current strategy keeps the church not just running in place, but falling further behind. We keep sending more and more people to leadership conferences but little seems to change. Why is there so little return on investment for all the dollars and time spent on conferences and seminars to help us do better? Because we are training mechanics to work on machinery of the church industry when we need a new engine. We are training leaders to address the leadership challenges of a world that is quickly passing away.

Past-Present Leadership Motifs

Church leaders in North America currently draw on several dominant motifs or metaphors for their understanding of the role and content of spiritual leadership. These have developed across the centuries. They emerged in response to specific leadership challenges. These models can be summed up in several categories (a more complete discussion of these can be found in Reggie McNeal, *Revolution in Leadership*, Abingdon Press, 1998). All these typically inform spiritual leaders as they fashion their own personal leadership philosophy.

Priest or Holy Person

Every religious tradition has people in it who understand its religious rites, can conduct its religious ceremonies, and can act as representatives of the divine. A priesthood emerged in Christianity very early and remains a powerful leadership function, both in Catholic and Protestant circles. The function of priests has shifted with the times. The role of the priest in dealing with mystery gained ascendancy throughout the early church and Middle Ages, whereas the role of today's priest involves the role of spiritual guide and mentor. The constant of these various functions is the role of the priest in representing God to people. This is why priests-clergy are sought out for weddings, funerals, christenings, prayer, and other special rites. Their connection to the divine creates value in them and gains them entrance to participate in life's key passages.

Shepherd or Pastor

This function of Christian leadership focuses on the caretaking aspect of spiritual leadership. In the Roman Catholic Church prior to the Reformation, the parish pastor was the curator of all souls residing in his geographic locale. In the Protestant world, this metaphor still provides significant content to the function of local congregational pastoral care. In many churches the shepherding is shared between clergy and lay leaders who serve the people in their church "flock" or church "family."

Educator or Wordsmith

The Renaissance and Reformation prompted the rise of this leadership function. The discovery of ancient documents (Greek and Hebrew manuscripts) fueled new learning. The pastor became the resident scholar for biblical studies. Textual exegesis became a prominent mode of dealing with Scripture. Enthusiasm for doctrinal issues reemerged as the church defined its way into the modern world, just as doctrinal debates had helped to establish the identity of the Christian movement in the first centuries of the church in the ancient world. The role of theologian, the educator, was garnered by the pastor, who frequently was the most educated person in the congregation. Leadership was afforded to the pastor in deference to his education and theological training. This position held true for years until the benefits of public education closed the gap on education between pulpit and pew. The pastor's position then changed to specialist for biblical and theological issues. With the rise of Christian publishing and media, even this distinction is collapsing. A leadership model based primarily on education now belongs to a previous world. Evidence for this is the growing number of congregations who view seminary education as an optional requirement for their pastors and church staff.

Managers or Program Directors

In the last half of the twentieth century church programming increased exponentially, due largely to the development of denominational programming and a proliferation of seminary-trained "educational" staff. Denominations produced programs and curriculums for every aspect of church life for every age group: Bible study, missions education, stewardship, discipleship, evangelism, family life, and so forth. Beginning in the 1970s, parachurch organizations began rivaling denominational publishing houses in the resources they produced and marketed to the local church. Accompanying resource kits were produced to ensure that lay leaders could administer these programs or teach the curriculum. In large churches these programs were coordinated and managed by staff leaders. The result was that church life became organized around major ministry programs (for example, Sunday School, Music Ministry, Women's Ministry). Lay leadership was tapped heavily to staff these programs. Other lay leadership resources were channeled into the burgeoning administration of the program-driven church.

Chief Executive Officer or Manager

With the rise of organizational life in American culture came the rise of management and management science, which has more recently morphed into the field of organizational behavior. The church has followed the complexifying trend of American organizational life, and the church leader has had to become at least minimally competent in the areas of personnel management, facilities planning, budgeting and fundraising, and program administration, to name a few. In more recent years the function of CEO became part of the leadership portfolio with the rise of megachurches with thousands of members with multiple million-dollar budgets situated on multimillion-dollar pieces of real estate. In recent years a range of executive positions have been added to these huge organizations (chief financial officer, chief operating officer, chief information officer, and so on) that attract thousands of worshipers each week. A study by the Lily Foundation recently found that half of all churchgoers in America attend the largest 10 percent of churches in the nation.

Leaders for these five leadership motifs have been trained and delivered to the church through a leadership pipeline that includes the prevailing church culture, Bible colleges, seminaries, and denominational training programs. All these leadership roles and functions continue to be useful in the church. People still need priests, shepherds, and biblical instruction. We need clergy and lay managers who can administrate church programs. Large congregations and megachurches need visionary leaders who can provide for the significant challenges endemic to large and complex organizations. And we need hospice chaplains for terminal congregations (there are thousands of them) who need someone to ease their pain in dying. (We also need estate planning for these congregations to endow kingdom growth!)

These leadership roles, however, are primarily geared for the current church culture. **We need transitional leaders who will help the church find a new expression in the emerging world.** What does this leadership look like and how will it be developed?

The Emergence of Apostolic Leadership

A new breed of church leader has been emerging that will meet the leadership challenges of what it will take for the church to become more missionally effective. In the last decades of the twentieth century, a new leadership genus began appearing on the North American church scene. This leadership type is what I and others have dubbed "apostolic leadership." This connotation seems appropriate primarily because the challenges to church leaders in the emerging twenty-first century parallel those that faced leaders in the first Christian century (commonly called the apostolic era). These include religious pluralism, globalism, and the collapse of institutional religion, accompanied by an increased interest in personal spiritual development. The focus of apostolic leadership is not on office or gifts (these are how people in the church culture deal with the term *apostle*), but on the content of leadership that responds to the new spiritual landscape by shaping a church movement that more resembles the world of Acts than America in the last half of the twentieth century.

I began to notice this new leadership animal in the 1980s, first as a participant and later as a presenter in church growth conferences sponsored by the Fuller Institute of Evangelism and Church Growth. A pattern developed. Fuller would go into a city to do a conference and attract several hundred high-octane, out-of-the-box types who were willing to try anything if it meant reaching more people with the gospel. These leaders were typically shunned by their denomination and other standard church leaders (this was before it was cool to be innovative). Looking back I can see clearly that God was raising up new leadership for the movement.

Apostolic leaders in the first and twenty-first centuries evidence distinctive characteristics. They are missional, meaning they order their lives around a missionary purpose. Apostolic leaders believe they are responsible for fulfilling the Great Commission. They are visionary; their efforts are energized by a vision of a preferred future, not just informed by a denominational program or the latest methodological fad. They are entrepreneurial, taking calculated risks to create markets for the gospel. Apostolic leaders prefer to work in teams. They plant churches in teams. They give leadership to existing churches in teams. They are not Lone Rangers. They often create and operate in what Warren Bennis calls "great groups." They release ministry to people and people for ministry. Their organizational "charts" (if they have them) are as flat as possible; they practice ad hocracy instead of establishing bureaucracy. They are genuinely spiritual. Their lives cannot be explained apart from the power of God. Apostolic leaders have a core value of cultural relevance. They come in both clergy and lay varieties.

Other leadership motifs require leaders to be competent to work inside the church. The apostolic leader's competency revolves around the ability to work outside the church in the

world that is not a part of the church culture. Even operating in a church position (as many do), apostolic leaders measure their effectiveness by their impact beyond the church walls. The other leadership motifs measure their effectiveness with church culture yardsticks. They ask themselves questions like: Was the service or church activity done well? Was the sermon or lesson well received? Are church programs staffed and operating with good customer satisfaction? Are the members taken care of in their time of need?

Apostolic leaders add to this list, at the top: Is anyone being brought into the kingdom? For them, even if all these other measures are showing high marks (and they are not unimportant to them) but no kingdom growth is occurring, they feel disobedient to the Great Commission. I am not suggesting that other leaders do not care about evangelism. Many do. However, it is possible to exercise previous leadership roles completely in the church bubble, and be considered successful in the church industry, while showing no significant kingdom growth. Apostolic leaders are all about kingdom growth, even in their pastoral care. (They will strategize on how to perform baby dedications for people who are not members as an outreach strategy.)

Who trains apostolic leaders? First and foremost, other apostolic leaders of "new tribe" churches. This group wants to learn from practitioners. Second, apostolic leaders learn a lot from the business culture. They study the business culture for reasons different from the leader's in the CEO-manager model. The latter wants the latest leadership or management insights to help him develop leadership skills in running the church operation. Apostolic leaders study business culture literature as a way to do cultural exegesis. Business leaders have to stay in touch with the culture to survive, so their insights inform apostolic leaders' entrepreneurial bent on developing ways of taking the gospel to the marketplace (where most people spend most of their time).

Seminary curriculum is designed primarily to address skill sets for leadership functions other than the apostolic type. Classical seminary training was birthed to service the wordsmith-educator function. It has focused on biblical education with a few practical courses thrown in to help students prepare for priestly functions (administering sacraments) and shepherding aspects of ministry (pastoral care, psychology, and so on). In recent decades some courses targeting church administration and leadership have been added.

Lay leaders are getting in on the apostolic leadership revolution. More and more people are entering ministry from all kinds of business backgrounds (the original apostles were small business owners). They are feeling the call of God on their life to be a part of kingdom expansion. Dennis left a much higher-salaried corporate position as a retirement community developer to become a local church pastor. Thomas sold his electrical business to develop a technical production company to resource student ministries. These leaders bring with them their corporate leadership training and life experience outside the church culture.

These apostolic leaders often view seminary as supplemental, not essential. Many are opting not to put on hold their plans for ministry while they go to seminary for three or four years. They read along the way, take on-line courses, and attach themselves to a new tribe mentor. This mentoring relationship is not necessarily personal. It may consist of mentorees reading the mentor's books, sermons, and visiting the mentor's church (in person or on-line). If they look to seminary it is not for leadership training but specialty information. They already have learned in life and business the things that seminarians complain "the seminary didn't teach me."

Going into full-time congregational ministry is only one way lay leaders are going apostolic. An increasing number of church members, desiring to see kingdom growth, are using their considerable personal and financial resources to develop or support ministries that target the community beyond the church walls.

More and more church leaders, clergy and lay, are moving toward the content of the apostolic model. I hear from pastors who are increasingly impatient with doing church. They are frustrated by club members who don't get it. I also hear from lay leaders who have far more vision than their pastors. They want to be a part of something significant and are growing discouraged waiting for the church (and their pastors) to catch up.

The journey to apostolic ministry is a difficult path for many, for some much like a deconversion. Shifting leadership gears in a typical church setting can lead to a lot of tension. One reason many spiritual leaders feel drawn into the church planting movement (sometimes called church multiplication) is, in part, to dodge some of this conflict. Other reasons include a growing impatience with business as usual, an urgency on the part of church leaders to reach people with the gospel, and a need to be part of something missionally effective, not just to preside over the status quo.

Apostolic leaders not only have leadership characteristics different from those of other leadership paradigms, they also develop differently. A leadership revolution requires a learning revolution to support it. This brings us to the tough question.

Tough Question: How Do We Develop Leaders for the Christian Movement?

I want to approach this question with two target groups in mind. First, we'll look at the clergy church leader who may discover he is more of an apostolic type of leader. What are the key competencies that need to be developed? What is the best way to develop these leadership competencies? A second group of leaders I have in mind are the lay leaders who themselves are part of the apostolic leadership movement. They are the missionary force in the marketplace. They are the heartbeat of renewal in North America. They are the future for the missional church. I find these people in every congregation I visit. They know something is wrong. They know God has more in mind for the Christian movement than they are typically experiencing at church. The local church pastor may not know these people. They may not even hold a church job (and they probably don't want one). How do we deliver to these missionaries just-in-time and already-in-place leadership development? How do we develop a leadership core that is not program based, but is instead a group of leaders who are ready to charge hell with a water pistol?

A Balanced Leadership Diet

Church program-based leadership development generally focuses on task management and the corresponding narrow range of competencies that are required to accomplish the assignment successfully. For instance, Sunday School teachers are usually trained in using curriculum, leading discussions, and employing teaching techniques. It is interesting that few are intentionally trained in how to study the Bible, so they rely on predigested material supplied to them by the curriculum developer or publisher. Very little development of leadership goes on. The focus is on functional capability of people in administrative and program roles defined by church culture expectations.

Leadership development that supports apostolic leadership and a missional renewal in the church pays attention to four arenas of learning: paradigm issues, microskill development, resource development, and personal growth. Each of these arenas is critical. All must be attended to.

Paradigm Issues (How Do You See Your World?)

How leaders view the world has a profound impact on their vision, values, and behaviors. The refuge paradigm, for instance, militates against church renewal. Many (some say most) churches are led by people who possess this view of the world. Paradigm issues play out in other areas. Legions of church leaders seem never to have heard of postmodernism and the challenges it presents to sharing the gospel. Many church leadership groups apparently have not grasped the insight that each generation now is a distinct culture and requires different leadership approaches. Most have never understood that the call to be missionaries means a shift from the member, business-as-usual approach to church life. The shift from "doing" church at the clubhouse to "being" church in the world is a paradigm shift that has apparently eluded many church leaders.

Many people in existing churches are willing to learn these new paradigms. Some of them already know them intuitively but have not been able to give language to their thoughts. Part of the reason I wrote this book was to help create conversations around these key issues. Until we do, our churches will continue to mire down in methodological debates and trivial pursuits.

We will never raise up a missionary force unless we challenge church leaders with issues of paradigm proportions. A telling sign of tentativeness and lack of self-esteem of the North American church shows up in its unwillingness to deal with topics that incite tension. Letting them struggle with the implications of the emerging new world is one of the sure signs of self-confidence. The willingness and ability of church leaders to talk intelligently and forthrightly about the emerging world will not *relativize* Christianity but will *relevantize* it.

Microskill Development

Skills for apostolic leaders to cultivate include vision cultivation and casting, communication, team building, change and transition leadership, mentoring and coaching, corporate culture management, conflict management and resolution, networking, project management, systems thinking, and interpersonal relationships, to name a few. (Note that these skills are not unique to apostolic leadership, but the content of apostolic leadership will drive how the skill is developed and why it is important.)

Microskill development is not limited to clergy. Having an effective missionary force will require that lay leader-missionaries know how to establish and conduct conversations about Jesus and the gospel with people in the workplace, how to develop relationships for the sake of the gospel, how to network believers in the marketplace for prayer and support, how to identify needs among coworkers, how to become prayer warriors in the office, how to become a life coach for people, how to develop Bible studies and seeker groups in the workplace and in the neighborhood, and how to refer people for various addictions, psychological needs, or emotional disorders. Notice that this skill set development has little to do with accomplishing church culture jobs.

Resource Development

A leader who does not know how to resource his work just produces ideas, not results. The key resources for spiritual leaders include prayer, people, time, money, facilities, and technology.

A church member culture will develop these resources quite differently from how a missionary culture would. Here's an overview of the distinction between the two cultures in how they approach resource development.

Resource: Prayer
      Member—praying for members, church program needs
      Missionary—praying for unchurched, outreach efforts
Resource: People
      Member—recruiting members into church activities
      Missionary—deploying into community
Resource: Time
      Member—finding time for church activities
      Missionary—creating time for mission expression
Resource: Money
      Member—raising money for club activities
      Missionary—channeling money to mission initiatives
Resource: Facilities
      Member—maintaining the clubhouse
      Missionary—seeking ways to move out into the community

Resource: Technology
   Member—supporting church ministries
   Missionary—creating ministry opportunities in the world

Let's develop each track a bit further. Here's what a typical resource training agenda might include for a leader of church activities:

Prayer
   Developing a prayer support team
   Developing a prayer ministry for team members
People
   Developing a ministry team
   Helping people discover and use spiritual gifts
Time
   Establishing church calendar policies and procedures
   Managing time for meetings and classroom functions
Money
   Developing and managing budget
   Overseeing stewardship education
Facilities
   Using room configuration for ministry objectives
   Understanding building use policies and procedures
   Housing church activities
Technology
   Using audio-visual support system for church
   Creating teaching aids
   Communicating with leadership team
   Using church Web site for support of ministry
   E-mailing members

Consider how different the resource training agenda might look for a missionary-leader who wants to share the gospel at work and sees this as his primary ministry.

Prayer

    Prayer-walking

    Raising prayer support

    Establishing a prayer ministry at work

    Praying for coworkers

    Journaling prayer

People

    Networking missionaries with a similar passion

    Building a ministry team

    Identifying and coaching talent in others

    Developing a team of support people for referral (therapists, counselors, and so forth)

Time

    Using life passages to establish relationships

    Calendaring events to coordinate with community calendar

    Recognizing key windows of openness to gospel

    Using lunchtime strategically

Money

    Raising money for counseling referrals

    Identifying community resources for financial assistance

    Offering financial planning seminars at work

Facilities

    Matching ministry activities with appropriate space

    Using personal home for prayer

    Creating sacred space at restaurants

    Establishing outdoor sanctuaries

    Making personal desk or office a ministry place

Technology

    Creating an e-mail ministry

    Tracking conversations

    Creating a ministry of encouragement

The lists are quite different in scope and in skill development. Which one of these two tracks do you think churches typically target for delivery? The member track, if at all. Let me say that I would be ecstatic if churches would even pay more attention to leadership development for church ministry needs. I believe it would raise the level of effectiveness of church ministry exponentially and help create a culture of excellence and responsiveness.

What would happen if churches decided to adopt the missionary training regimen? First off, the staff would probably need to make an admission that seminary training didn't prepare them to equip people for missionary service. The best resources for training probably are missionary-practitioners from your own church or from another church that is doing this type of work.

Personal Growth

The issues in this arena of development between apostolic clergy and lay leaders are different and the same. Some items, such as practicing spiritual disciplines, are similar no matter what the leadership venue. Some issues, however, are significantly affected by the scope of ministry assignment.

A compendium of personal growth items would include personal spiritual disciplines, talent identification and development, family relationships (beginning with family of origin issues), emotional health, financial health, personal mission clarification, avoidance of behavior that leads to ministry derailment, leadership dragons (loneliness, anger, and so on), and finishing well. All of these issues aim at improving the leader's grasp of the most important piece of information he has: self-understanding.

Imagine that leaders of your church felt that, because they had taken leadership assignments, they were positioned to receive the benefit of investigating the above topics for their own lives. They would feel cared for at a profound level. Do you think such an environment would be one where people would have to be begged to serve in leadership capacities? I don't think so. Do you think leaders would feel used, underappreciated, burned out? I don't think so. Do you think the atmosphere would be different, with a jazzed-up group of leaders? I think so, too.

A leadership regimen like this might also attract some people you currently consider to be in the "fringe" or "uncommitted" categories in your church. I believe you have people like this in your church, waiting for something or someone to call them to a passionate mission beyond the typical church program.

You might also attract some real bona fide community leaders, businesspeople, and marketplace citizens who may or may not be connected to your church who may become interested in something you are doing. Some leadership resources in your community will be drawn to you if you get outside the walls. I had lunch one day with an attorney in Montgomery, Alabama. He told me that he attends an inner-city church, not because he lives in the city (he lives in a suburb) but because this inner-city church has an active ministry to the community. "I want to make a contribution to the community where I work," he explained.

A Leadership Learning Community

The goal of a congregation's leadership development process is to create a core of leaders who are capable of strategizing, launching, and conducting a mission for expanding the kingdom of God. Contrast this to holding a leadership role in an organization that primarily makes demands of the leaders' time, money, talents, energy, and prayer for its own survival. This shift will require significant changes both in attitude and behavior in leaders. It will not be a small feat to accomplish, especially because the current mental models and behavioral patterns for the role and content of leadership have been deeply engrained over several generations to focus only inward on the church.

I am talking about nothing less than a leadership revolution. What is our best shot for pulling off a leadership revolution? What is the delivery system for developing leaders for the missional renewal of the North American church? The answer: learning communities.

The power of learning in community is undeniable. The first and most elemental lessons we learn in life we learn in community: our family of origin. We have spent the rest of our lives either building on these lessons or trying to get over them! The power of learning in community is appreciated and used by behavior modification groups and recovery groups. Weight Watchers, Alcoholics Anonymous, and groups like them understand that most people need the support of a group in order to make significant behavioral shifts in their lives.

I suggest you consider two manifestations of learning community in developing apostolic leadership that leads to your experiencing Christianity as a movement. You need both organic and organizational community. You can fuse the two.

Organic Community

The organic community is the most critical aspect in shifting or shaping the corporate culture of your ministry. This was the primary approach used by Jesus. He lived with his disciples. This allowed him to debrief their lives and ministry assignments. In effect, he taught them how to learn from life and ministry. He sent the Holy Spirit to be their ongoing coach when he ascended back to the Father. The Book of Acts reveals how the learning community Jesus established shaped the movement (they continued to learn when surprised by the growth of the kingdom).

Establishing learning community involves developing a heart-to-heart, life-to-life relationship that will support mutual accountability, the capacity to challenge each other's biases and assumptions, and the freedom to assess results and spiritual growth. Some sort of small group dynamic will be required.

The power of the culture at large and the church culture to keep us in old systems is overwhelming without the support of others. I am not suggesting that you have to live with your missional community, but you might feel that way! Many missional leadership groups are in contact almost daily. At the very least, if you are in a congregational setting, you must find ways to connect the hearts of the leadership corps, not just train them for their assignment. I think this is more critical than any other function. I would quit anything else to accomplish this. Less will be more.

A word to pastors. Over time there is no substitute for your leadership inner circle to be in some small group setting with you where your heart for the kingdom can have an impact on theirs. (I believe this is the primary responsibility for church leaders: to share God's heart with God's people.) This means that you turn your board into a small group learning community first. Secondarily, they have responsibility for board decisions.

Organizational Community

What would a leadership learning community that is organizational in scope look like in a local congregation? I recommend a strategy that involves establishing affinity-based learning clusters that convene a minimum of once a month around the leadership issues I've outlined above. The affinities would probably center around ministry assignment (youth small group leaders) or passion (missionaries to multihousing complexes). The shape of the training and development sessions can adopt any one of at least three scenarios. Each scenario will involve some component of vision casting, microskill development, and cluster sharing.

Scenario One. A monthly churchwide leadership community meeting is convened by the senior pastor. In the large group setting the senior pastor does about fifteen minutes of vision casting about the mission of the church (this probably will consist of success stories about where the vision is being lived out). Someone (either the pastor, staff member, or person with specific expertise) conducts a training session of around forty-five minutes dealing with one of the topics I've already identified. The training session then breaks up into clusters for specific application, prayer, and ministry preparation. In a year's time the training session visits all four of the leadership development arenas (paradigm shifts, microskill development, resource development, and personal growth).

Scenario Two. This scenario is a modification of the first one. Monthly leadership community gatherings are convened by leaders other than the senior pastor (staff age group coordinators, committee chairs, for example). Vision casting, leadership development, and cluster time are handled just as in scenario one. The "tribal" leader who convenes the meetings acts as learning coach to the clusters in their leadership constellation. A churchwide leadership community is convened by the senior pastor once a quarter.

Scenario Three. Leadership development is done primarily in the clusters, with only quarterly gatherings of a larger leadership community. Training topics are delivered to the clusters either through video, CD-ROM, or the Internet. Vision casting is handled between large group gatherings through e-mail updates and testimonials of ministry success.

Leadership will determine the shape of the Christian movement as we move into the third Christian millennium. Leadership will decide whether we follow the path of the Pharisees to oblivion (by practicing a refuge brand of Christianity) or reemerge as a vibrant church that has the requisite energy to spark personal and community transformation. **The call to apostolic leadership is God's answer to the challenges to the Christian movement in North America.** The emergence and development of this new kind of leader provides hope for the future and a way forward into renewal.

I am frequently asked, "Can I become an apostolic leader even if I started somewhere else in my leadership journey?" My answer is "yes." It will take enormous courage and a willingness to travel a steep unlearning curve. You will have to be willing to change behavior, not just your vocabulary and reading list. It's not everyone's call, but if you feel pulled to it by God you will never find fulfillment short of pursuing it.

The rise of apostolic leadership is a revolution already under way. Consider this your invitation to join!

Things I Didn't Say

Often when I am speaking to a group I feel there should be a large plasma screen suspended over my head with a running commentary on what I am *not* saying. Some people in the audience hear some of what I say, but because I don't use code words they are looking for or phrases they are used to hearing (church-speak), they begin filling in blanks with things I didn't say or mean to say. Or they hear one of my hyperbolic statements and freak out. Then they shut down and miss the point (and a lot of the points following). Occasionally people hear exactly what I am saying and disagree with me. In those cases I think one of two things: either they didn't quite get it or they are of the devil (I'm just teasing—mostly).

So in an effort for clarity, or as a final act of persuasion (since I know you will agree with me once you fully understand what I am saying), I am offering the print version of that imaginary screen that should hang over my head like a bubble in the cartoon strips. Here is what you may have thought you heard me say, or wondered whether I said, but did *not* hear me say.

It's Over for the Church

I did not say that it's over for the church. **What I did say is that unless significant shifts occur in attitudes and practices, the institutional church in North America is in deep trouble—and**

it should be, because it has lost its mission. Most people in church cannot think about Christianity apart from its institutional expression, so their faith is in for a rough ride as the church culture continues to decline. Most church leaders think that renewal has something to do with institutional revival, but this misses the point. The Christian movement in its next phase will be more missional, less institutional, and more in the street, and it will not conform to our current notions of what church should be like. But it will be the church of Jesus. And it is going to be a significant part of the spiritual landscape for America.

Many individual congregations and church leaders understand this and are pursuing an aggressive strategy of partnering with God in his redemptive mission in the world. They will thrive. When people in the new movement of kingdom growth look for a tribe to be a part of, they will find their way to one of the congregations or groups that get it.

A lot of religious clubs (currently called churches) will continue to operate just fine—for a while, maybe a long while, depending on how well they build and manage their endowment. It is quite possible that we will have a good number of churches being financed by dead people. As long as missionless churches maintain financial support, they can remain in their denial and self-delusion that they are the Christian movement in North America.

We Need a Postmodern Church

I did not say that we need a postmodern church, nor did I say we need for the church to pursue its understanding of the culture in order to mimic it. The last thing we need is a postmodern church. We need a church for postmodern people (like we've had a church for people in the centuries of modernity). **The reason to get in touch with the culture is not to adopt it but to engage it for the same reasons a missionary does—in order to gain a hearing for the gospel.** I am not enamored by the culture, but I am responsible for the Great Commission. The people who want to debate my points about cultural relevance are not motivated by the Great Commission. They are monoculturalists who practice spiritual imperialism. Their evangelism efforts are really an inverted refuge mentality (we'll hide from the world by turning the world into being like us).

Christianity and Spirituality Are the Same

I did not say that Christianity and spirituality are the same. **What I did say is that a spiritual hunger is fueling an awakening to God.** The expression of this new spirituality is certainly not all Christian; in fact, much of it is not. We are currently in an ecumenism that celebrates "people of faith" as if all faith is based in truth. I am pleading with followers of Jesus to seize the moment and use this new spiritual openness to create conversations that will introduce people to Jesus, who *is* truth.

There Are Ways to God Besides Jesus

I have discovered through the years that once I champion cultural relevance and the ability to have conversations with people outside the church bubble, it becomes necessary to defend my orthodoxy. It is easier for some people to relegate me to heresy than to deal with the issues I raise. I am particularly nervous about this charge. I know what the church has done to heretics. It's not dying that's scary. It's what they do to you before they let you die that frightens me.

Jesus said that God draws people to himself. And he also said that he was a part of this process ("I, when I am lifted up from the earth, will draw all men to myself" John 12:32, NIV). God draws people to himself through Jesus, who is the way. **People may and do begin their spiritual journeys from many starting points, but truth ultimately converges at one door, one path, and one life— Jesus.** He is the only hope for salvation, for he alone is the Incarnation of God in human flesh. His nature as God, along with his sacrificial visit to this planet, gives him the right to set the rules. He says no one comes to the Father except through him. That is an exclusive claim, and it is offensive to people who are busy working their way to God on their own terms. The cross is always offensive, in every culture and in every generation, because it is the reminder that humans are in need of salvation and can't do anything about it except on God's terms. This claim of exclusivity cost the early Christians their lives. It will stick in the throat of a religiously plural twenty-first century world just as it did in the first century.

All Churches Should Be Contemporary

I did not say that all churches should be contemporary. When some people hear me talking about being culturally conversant, they immediately jump to this conclusion. I don't like the label *contemporary* anyway, because what is contemporary today will not be contemporary five years from now. What I have said is that each culture must worship God in its own heart language. This applies to generational cultures as well as ethnic cultures, and it means that expressions of the church will shift as it engages different cultures.

Does this mean that the traditional church is dead? Of course not. Plenty of people prefer traditional, but you will continue to see more traditional elements of church incorporated into new forms. The key is the presence of mission. **Missionless religion that calls itself Christianity is an affront to God, however it styles itself.**

Bible Study Is Not Important

I never said that Bible study is unimportant. Every follower of Jesus who is interested in knowing God better wants to study the Bible. We are privileged to have the Scriptures.

The current dilemma with how we use the Bible is twofold. One is that in the last gasps of the modern church, we have made Bible study in itself a mark of spiritual maturity, clearly missing the major evidences of what God looks for in his search for spiritual maturity—our relationship to him and to people. The Pharisees studied the Scripture and knew it better than any other group, but Jesus chided them for missing the point. (He was the point!) **If our Bible study does not show up in a life that looks increasingly like Jesus' (captured by his heart for people), it is merely a head trip, a point of pride, and an idolatrous substitute for genuine spirituality.** Second, in a pluralistic religious environment, we need to remember that it is not essential for people to convert to the Bible; it is imperative that they meet Jesus and begin to develop a relationship with him. When a person loves Jesus, that person will want to know everything Jesus did and said. This hunger to know him more will naturally lead to the Bible. People do not need to agree with our definition of the truth to come to the Truth.

I Am Against Planning

I didn't say that I'm against planning, but I am against a lot of the planning that goes on in churches, because it pushes the present into the future and secures the continued pitiful state of most churches in terms of missional vibrancy. What I did say is that there is a dimension of futuring that goes beyond planning. I call this spiritual preparation, and I have detailed the five components of a spiritual preparation architecture: vision, values, results, strengths, and learnings. Planning is an appropriate activity for the deployment of resources (people, time, money, facilities, prayer, technology). **Preparation enables you to catch the wave of God's activity by living in an attitude of obedience to the redemptive mission of God in the world.**

These Shifts Will Be Easy

I know you didn't think that I said this, but I just threw it in so I could say something else. If this stuff were easy it would have been done already. These shifts, though under way, will be resisted by many who prefer to default to business-as-usual church life. Entire congregations will regrettably capitulate to the loud cries of a few who stand in the way of the church's participating in this future. **It takes enormous courage to give spiritual leadership in the North American church culture, because the church is increasingly hostile to anything that disturbs its comfort and challenges its club member paradigm.** What I did say is that the persecution of Christian leaders in North America comes from inside the church, from club members. It will grow more intense in the years ahead.

The Situation Is Hopeless

I definitely did not say that the situation is hopeless. What I did say is that **it's later than you think.** The missional renewal of the North American church is essential to its future. I am convinced that most expressions of the institutional church in America will not survive the emerging world. If that sounds threatening to you, then you may be more in love with the church than you are with Jesus. You need to take this up with him.

I believe Jesus is the hope of the world. I believe God has called out a people to make sure the world knows this. These people are the church. Jesus has promised that hell will not be able to stand against it.

I just wish hell were the problem.

Conclusion

He had tears in his eyes. "Until I met you I thought I was crazy." He is a pastor who gets it, who is turning an old rural church in the middle of nowhere inside out. It's a church no one has ever heard of, except the people who are finding Jesus there. "Of course," he laughed, "it could just be that both of us are crazy."

That young pastor may be right. But he and thousands like him and tens of thousands of church members are the people I wrote this book for. These are good souls who yearn to see Pentecost come to North America, to see God move in our time in ways that sweep across the landscape and change it. People who have given their lives to the church believing this has been obedience to God but now wondering whether obedience will lead them out of church and into the streets. Followers of Jesus who are convinced that his life and death must not be squandered on an institution that seeks and saves those who are . . . saved.

As I said in the Introduction I am not the only person who has these views or has written them down. I have friends with whom I've talked who share my perspectives. Some of them you would recognize, but I won't embarrass them by linking them with my polemics.

But I have felt a unique calling in all this turbulence. Unlike some writers I am not a practitioner in one church setting with a particular model of church to propose. And I am more than a commentator who studies and tracks trends in the North American culture that the church must reckon with. **My role, because of my life calling, is to help leaders who are practitioners in many different settings sort through the implications of an emerging world in terms of how we *are* church.** I have sought to give a theological, not just a methodological, rationale for reimagining the church in North America. I believe the central doctrine for missional renewal is the biblical teaching on the priesthood of all believers, the people of God called out and empowered to join him in his redemptive mission in the world. I have added the phrase "in the world" every time I have referenced God's redemptive mission, because the church in our culture has forgotten to look for God there, instead believing that the church is the primary scope of the work of God. Nothing less than dying to ourselves will free us from ourselves so we can come alive to God and become captured by his heart for people who don't know him yet.

I would hope to succeed in helping you see that much of what you are consumed with (if you are a typical church leader) is destined to be discarded. If I have failed it's in not choosing words compelling enough for you to see just how the future is changing everything, how the new realities are reframing the Christian movement. The birth of the kingdom age under way may be the drawing of the net, or it may be a new way the church relates to the world for the next five hundred years. I could perhaps have been more tentative, more tender, and more solicitous in places. I just don't want you or me to be left standing at the gate after the flight has departed.

One thing is for sure. God is not struggling with these changes. None of this catches him off guard or ill prepared. His purposes will be accomplished just as sure as you will finish reading this sentence. The future for him is already present. He calls out from that future to his people. He wants us to join him where he is.

We all know the episode during Passion Week involving Jesus and that fruitless fig tree (Matthew 21:18–22; Mark 11:12–14,

20–24), commonly referred to as the cursing of the fig tree. Two things about that story bothered me for years. First, why did Jesus pick on that poor fig tree? Nowhere else does he take out his frustration on nature. I also wondered about the teaching on prayer associated with this event. It's like Jesus was saying, "If you believe, you can fry fig trees, too."

I eventually consulted a "figologist" (sort of) who helped me see what was going on here. Not only was this tree not supposed to have fruit at this time of the year (this point is even made in the Mark account), it wasn't supposed to have leaves either. This tree was acting out! It was one sick puppy. It was badly out of rhythm. The fig tree was already dying. Jesus knew this. The miracle of the story is not the demise of the tree but how fast it happened. Jesus fast-forwarded the future. By the way, the disciples knew the tree was dying, too. They didn't exclaim, "You killed that fig tree!" Rather, they asked, "How did you do that so quickly?"

Once I understood the miracle I understood Jesus' teaching on prayer. He tells us that if we can see things the way they really are (not just the way they appear), we can partner with God through prayer in fast-forwarding the future.

This book is my prayer. I am convinced God wants a better future for the church in North America. If we can begin asking the right questions, I believe we can partner with him in bringing it about.

Now, let us pray.

References

New Reality Number One

Barna, George. *The State of the Church 2002*. Ventura, Calif.: Issachar Resources, 2002, p. 14.

Barna, George, *The State of the Church 2002*, pp. 12–17.

Bird, Craig. "Pastors Says, 'Post-Congregationals Leaving Church, but Not Their Faith." *Associated Baptist Press*, October 30, 2002, Volume 02–102.

"Charting America's Religious Landscape." http://www.csmonitor. com/2002/1010/p12s01-lire.html. October 10, 2002.

"New Research Casts More Doubt on Church Attendance Figures." http://www.atheists.org/flash.line/church1.htm. August 2, 2002.

Rainer, Thom. "Attendance Stats by Generation." Private e-mail message to Reggie McNeal, 12/12/02.

New Reality Number Six

McNeal, Reggie. *Revolution in Leadership*. Nashville, Tenn.: Abingdon Press, 1998.

The Author

Dr. *Reggie McNeal* enjoys helping people, leaders, and Christian organizations pursue more intentional lives. He currently serves as the Missional Leadership Specialist for Leadership Network of Dallas, Texas. His past experience involves over a decade as a denominational executive and leadership development coach. He also served in local congregational leadership for over twenty years, including being the founding pastor of a new church. Reggie has lectured or taught as adjunct faculty for multiple seminaries, including Fuller Theological (Pasadena, California), Southwestern Baptist (Ft. Worth, Texas), Golden Gate Baptist (San Francisco, California), Trinity Divinity School (Deerfield, Illinois), and Columbia International (Columbia, South Carolina). In addition, he has served as a consultant to local church, denomination, and para-church leadership teams, as well as seminar developer and presenter for thousands of church leaders across North America. He has also served as a resource for the United States Army Chief of Chaplains Office, Air Force chaplains, and the Air Force Education and Training Command. McNeal's work also extends to the business sector, including The Gallup Organization.

He has contributed to numerous denominational publications and church leadership journals, including *Leadership* and *Net Results*. His books include *Revolution in Leadership* (Abingdon Press, 1998),

A *Work of Heart: Understanding How God Shapes Spiritual Leaders* (Jossey-Bass, 2000), *Practicing Greatness* (Jossey-Bass, 2006), *Get A Life!* (Broadman & Holman, 2007) and *Missional Renaissance: Changing the Scorecard for the Church* (Jossey-Bass, 2009).

McNeal's education includes a B.A. degree from the University of South Carolina and the M.Div. and Ph.D. degrees both from Southwestern Baptist Theological Seminary.

McNeal and his wife, Cathy, have two daughters, Jessica and Susanna, and make their home in Columbia, South Carolina.

The Present Future DVD Collection

Six Tough Questions for the Church, Set

Reggie McNeal

ISBN 978-0-7879-8673-5

Join Reggie McNeal in person in this lively video presentation, based on his best-selling book, **The Present Future: Six Tough Questions for the Church**. In this ten-session four-DVD curriculum you will accompany best-selling author Reggie McNeal and his studio audience as they explore the six most important new realities that church leaders must face as they are to move beyond "churchianity" to a more authentic and missional Christian faith. By changing the questions church leaders ask themselves about their congregations and their mission, they can reshape the Christian movement in North America, acknowledge generational shifts, and provide stimulating new ways of thinking about the missional possibilities of the church.

The package includes 1 Leader's guide, 1 Participant's guide, and 4 DVDs.

Filmed live before a studio audience, with Reggie McNeal teaching in his own distinctive style, the ten sessions include:

o **Session One: "Preparing for the Future"**—a conversation designed to raise the possibility of experiencing a spiritual awakening and its implications for believers and the church

o **Session Two: "What Are You Looking At?"**—the DVD series introduction that challenges participants to turn their attention to the world around them

o **Session Three: "The Collapse of the Church Culture,"
Part One**—a session that examines the impact on the
church of the rise of distinct generational cultures in
North America

o **Session Four: "The Collapse of the Church Culture,"
Part Two**—a discussion that confronts participants with
the reality that getting back to the Christian movement
will require a deconversion from "churchianity"

o **Session Five: "From Church Growth to Kingdom
Growth"**—a shift that moves our agenda from building
great churches to serving our communities

o **Session Six: "A New Reformation: Releasing God's
People"**—a way of thinking that turns church members
into missionaries and requires that they be freed from
church involvement

o **Session Seven: "The Return to Spiritual Formation"**—
the need to address a fundamental need to help people
grow as people, not just better church members

o **Session Eight: "From Planning to Preparation"**—a look
at how churches must move beyond incremental thinking
(the result of planning more of the same) into partnering
with God in his redemptive mission in the world (the
result of a spiritual preparation modality when getting
ready for the future)

o **Session Nine: "The Rise of Apostolic Leadership"**—the
reality of leadership requirements for spiritual leaders in a
world that resembles A.D.30

o **Session Ten: "What's Next?"**—an exploration of what
next steps might be taken by believers and churches to
align themselves with God's future for them